A **HUMAN**, THEN A **BUILDING**, NOW A **RISING STOCK**

Berry Beans

Tampa, Florida

The contents of this work, including, but not limited to, the accuracy of events, people, and places depicted; opinions expressed; permission to use previously published materials included; and any advice given or actions advocated are solely the responsibility of the author, who assumes all liability for said work and indemnifies the publisher against any claims stemming from publication of the work.

All Rights Reserved
Copyright © 2024 by Berry Beans

No part of this book may be reproduced or transmitted, downloaded, distributed, reverse engineered, or stored in or introduced into any information storage and retrieval system, in any form or by any means, including photocopying and recording, whether electronic or mechanical, now known or hereinafter invented without permission in writing from the publisher.

Published by Gatekeeper Press
7853 Gunn Hwy., Suite 209
Tampa, FL 33626
www.GatekeeperPress.com

Paperback ISBN: 9781662952371
eISBN: 9781662952388

A **HUMAN**, THEN A **BUILDING**, NOW A **RISING STOCK**

The story I am about to tell you, are based on shocking but true events surrounding my life. This story is about losses I endured during years of my life but through losses I have risen to overcome addiction and continue to move forward in life. Further involves a city with possible corruption.

July 5th, 2008, was the last time my family and I saw my brother alive. Remembering that day, I wanted to hang out with him since it would be his last day alive; he said no but should have pushed harder. At one time, I did blame myself, but it's only natural when losing a loved one, especially if it is unexpected. One day he was here, and the next day he was taken away from us forever. I don't understand why I never got to see his body or why no one got me that night. I was only seventeen always did things to win his approval or please him. The last person to be with James when he was alive is his friend Marcus.

According to reports on July 6th at 12:16 a.m. my older brother, James Alan Beri, was struck and killed instantly by Joshua as they claimed him to be a drunk driver from Carrington, North Dakota. Routine firework shows took place on the fourth that day they rescheduled to the fifth. Rumors, facts, or the truth was he plus a friend were riding bikes out towards the pasta plant to light off some fireworks. Marcus claimed they were out there to light off some kind of a bomb. My brother was in the military. James may have had some knowledge involving bombs. If true. It would open the door for a Federal Investigation, which made me interested that he said that.

James Alan Beri Born: 18 Dec 1987 Department of Veterans Affairs
Died: 6 Jul 2008 Military Service
Carrington Cemetery **PRIVATE**
Unnamed Rd US ARMY
Carrington, Foster, North Dakota IRAQ WAR

As far as I know of any witnesses that would have known is Marcus, Joshua, and an unknown guy that someone claims was with Josh the night he was killed or if the police collected any evidence.

Conversation: I know who was with him that night in his pickup with him when he killed him, man. If you wanna know come 2 my house in nrf. Nrf aka New Rockford.

I never did go to her house in New Rockford even though I was curious but paranoid and/or cautious due to what I have seen, read, and experienced. Hearsay was that Joshua went to my soon-to-be friend's house (Bonnie's trailer house) where he walked to the back where there was a campfire going while fleeing the scene must have been a rumor and/or he was a fast runner and/or slow reaction of police response. A state trooper of North Dakota lived close to the crime scene and/or accident. A comment my mom made was the state trooper heard it over the radio, so he did respond but was not requested to do so. Did this make a difference or not? There was an audio report of a 911 call made by the suspect stating he may have hit a deer. I attempted to get the original records of the case involving my brother's death. The lawyer told me over the phone that records were no longer available destroyed. Maybe the case is closed? I was not satisfied with the outcome but escalated more suspicion. I lost that battle, but now the pictures, the lawyer told me that my mom had to give permission, which was granted but still, I failed to obtain them.

What is further disturbing is my brother's friend Marcus never got a scratch. If two people are best friends riding bikes together, they would be riding side by side or front to back. None of it makes any sense, just more questions than answers surrounding this alleged accident or crime. Hearsay was a city male police officer who was first on the scene, described as running around panicking like a chicken with his head cut off. I will remind you there was a state cop living straight across from the trailer park and a mile or so away from this questionable accident. I began to conduct an investigation myself.

When I woke up that day at my friend Elmer's place ten blocks away from the trailer court, I received texts asking if I was okay and a call from my mom asking for me to come home right away. Wondering what was happening, I headed back to the trailer park on foot. As I got to the mailboxes outside, a guy drove up saying not to worry Joshua would receive proper and/or fair justice, but how would he be able to guarantee that? I remember the day like it happened yesterday. After I learned what happened, I am not sure what my reaction was, but I remember my employer calling.

Cowboy Pizza calling interrupting the deliverance of bad news asking me into work. That is when something hit and I broke down crying trying to explain to him what happened then hanging up and/or handing phone to my mom. After that, I was running away mentally but physically walking back over to Elmer's to drink the pain away and break the news to him.

The manager of Cowboy Pizza gave me a few days after something like that happening my brother was taken away from me only a few days was not enough nor did I return to work. I never experienced anything like this before and I was only seventeen at the time. I got dependent and/or escalated on my drinking of alcohol never wanted to be sober again and face reality. The funeral followed after I remember my father saying he wouldn't show up at his own funeral. I was debating whether I should go or not. I ended up going but attended under the influence my niece wanted a drink of my pop said no because it was a mix. After the suspicions of drinking were confirmed.

Shortly after my brother got killed, I lashed out on random people's property and discovered the five-finger discount at one location where a manager would follow me around as I window-shopped. After a short period I targeted people that I felt were involved, connected and those that held my brother in contempt deserved my wrath. One of the many people had a camper parked in front of Elmer's that was my usual spot, so they felt my fury because how dare they occupy MY parking space. I didn't know how else to act or express myself. One person that held my brother in contempt got her cage rattled that night claiming he committed suicide. I remember banging on her windows with a wrench and then throwing the same solid brick into her tailor multiple times because it would not stay in place. The only reason I would regret this act is she was renting the trailer.

People underestimate how hard it is to move on after such a tragic loss, the pain I felt in my heart was like shooting a cannon through it. The only thing that kept me alive was knowing how much sorrow I would create with my demise by having my mom bury not one but two of her children. My brother Alex wouldn't understand why we would have never spoken again. My little sister Amanda would likely blame herself for my death wondering why I did it. I believe I have not been able to move past this tragic loss because of the lack of justice and no closure. I was able to hide, cover, and distract from it or maybe I was just fooling myself and/or people saw it but ignored it. While in treatment my shrink Ben would claim I used laughing or joking as a distraction or a way to avoid being questioned was he right? After the loss, I didn't know how to act normally, but it hasn't only changed my life forever.

The death affected family members, including my parents. My father was tough. He was always working on getting justice, communicating with lawyers, state, and/or federal agents but passed away in 2012, which will be explained later on. My mom at one time said it was like living in a twilight zone she is still currently alive but endured a lot of turmoil through life starting in Rapid City, South Dakota, where most of us were born, involving custody battles with us kids. She also joined the Marines but never finished basic training. Reason for joining was her boyfriend was caught with another woman; he then discouraged her from joining so she wanted to either prove him wrong or get away from the area. She shared this with me, but the only detail she gave was her being under the influence at the time. If I would have known sooner growing up and/or been educated better on how the system worked in life, things might have been different. I believe education is important growing up, especially at a young age to what you'd expect or enter into. I like to think of life as a war; you win and lose battles, so it's better to be prepared than to enter into an ambush.

My older sister firstborn Stephine also served in the military, meeting her husband in the service, had three kids with him, but now the father has custody of all of them all. She was in the process of getting her tubes tied, but the doctors informed her that she was already pregnant because of this, she chose to name him after our late brother thinking it was meant to happen. The story is conflicting on what happened to her mental health, whether it was seizures, drugs, mental breakdown, or something happened that took place between her and the father of her kids in St. Joseph, Missouri. I have not done any investigation into it YET, but it was tough for me to struggle through life, whether that sounds selfish and/or an excuse, but they do say you gotta help yourself before helping others. The second brother is Alex, he's mentally challenged, so not sure if he was affected or not.

James was the third one born. He dropped out of high school and took his General Educational Development, then joined the US Army. A few memories I have of him are Army related. He was so excited to go that he forgot to take his drug test at our home in New Rockford. Another one was meeting him and picking him up from a hotel in Fargo. He smiled and pretended he didn't know me. I was the fourth one born and considered or felt like the runt of the family growing up. I considered myself below-average growing up but now I am in the lead among my family in life.

My younger brother fifth-born, Cookie, ended up getting into drugs. Not sure what kind, but my best guess would be Synthetic Marijuana, Bath Salts, Meth, and/or combinations of them all. He was dating a girl named Karen, but after he broke up with her, he has not been the same to the point where his lights were on but no one was home. I remember me and a family friend, Big D, talking my mom into calling the police to get him some help because he was burning stuff inside of our trailer house, but police did nothing, claiming he was not breaking the law, but he was a danger to himself and/or others by lighting stuff on fire, like money for some reason. I feel I've lost him at a mental capacity but physically still here. At one time my mom stood in front of a car that my brother was driving hoping he would get out. He proceeded to drive forward. No one was hurt.

Amanda last born she was only eleven at the time; never really asked her about how she felt then or now about it but got a feeling she wouldn't wanna answer or talk about it. She currently is in a relationship with an abusive, controlling estranged boyfriend. I did do my best to help her to the point of advising her to leave him for good, but she claimed at the time she was in love with him. I have been between their fights, which involved a lot of destruction and was like a tornado going through their place. Her boyfriend is built stocky and both of them have bad tempers.

I thought about reaching out to family and others for piecing my life or writing together, but I have failed to so with maintaining secrecy at this same time. I am one that never got in or addicted to drugs except for the cough syrup Robitussin for a short time while living in Bismarck, North Dakota. I would take about forty to sixty pills at a time. Passing out a few times while outside Robo-tripping and/or Robo walking.

I remember waking up outside next to a pickup. I have experienced smoking weed, which never mixed well with drinking didn't like the dry throat and/or cough that came with it. Drinking was my choice of drug. When growing up, my outlook of a normal life was finishing high school, college, a good job, getting married, and having kids, but it ain't what they call an American dream or a reality of life. You can either plan it out, but from my experience, it never goes as planned reasoning for myself going with the flow.

Dropped out of high school reason and/or excuse was the principal came up behind me, putting me in some kind of chokehold during some study hall time being held in the lunchroom. I remember staring into this girl's eyes getting locked and lost in them never had the confidence at the time to ask her out, though. Felt she was too pretty or hot for me. Whether it sounds silly, that's how I felt. I was considered or labeled as a member in the nerd herd group as other students called it but soon gained more popularity.

At the time I thought college was a waste of time, money, and/or a scam if I was to do it over again. I would be a police officer, lawyer, and/or something along the lines of investigation. Police only detain arrest and charge people for the crimes they commit after that it's up to the lawyers to prosecute. Working in both areas would give you more knowledge to better assist or understand both fields as they should be equal to each other. I've had a few good jobs I have enjoyed but self-sabotaged them. The job titles were shop assistant at a scrapyard in Dickinson, produce item picker at a produce warehouse in Jamestown, and an unload-er for incoming trucks at Walmart in St. Joseph, Missouri. While employed with Walmart I have worked in several different areas with the favorite one was unloading items on pallets then later moving them to the floor job ending in Jamestown, North Dakota.

I never imagined myself getting married and/or planned it out nor did I have a smooth game is what they would call it. If anything, I am or was a shy gentleman. I was working on confidence and asserting myself. Low self-esteem, confidence, and/or motivation all played roles in myself being single. Would I change it? Everything happens for a reason. I don't think anyone ever expects an ambush or is prepared to enter into life on their own after their eighteenth birthday. Compared to education back then and now, students are even less prepared without learning life's basic skills, like for example how to address an envelope and where stamps are supposed to be placed. Another one is not knowing basic vehicle maintenance like checking or changing the oil and/or putting a spare tire on the vehicle.

Greed is the root of all evil. This is where the courts come in. The guy that took my brother away forever had a well-known name, was an upstanding member of the community, a background as a firefighter, money, and a power house attorney—you would still think fair justice, correct? Your wrong the same night the killing took place he may have bailed out the same day like it was nothing, so the police and courts thought he was a deer too? When he was an Iraq veteran who served his country.

An insult from the courts and/or an injustice in the making? You will find out as the story continues down below is a news article and a list of original charges filed. You will notice that there is no specific class of charges and/or people involved listed in the news article below. The article is too thin and lacks important information to the general public; but why? News outlets lacked the ability to care and/or maybe police withheld information? Either way, should've raised a lot of questions not only for me but the general public as well.

> CARRINGTON, N.D. - A 20-year-old Carrington man has been charged in Foster County District Court in connection with a traffic incident Sunday that left another Carrington man dead. Charges against Joshua Alan Sherman include manslaughter, escape, leaving the scene of an accident involving death, and being in actual physical control of a vehicle while impaired.

Sherman was driving a pickup on a gravel road about 12:15 a.m. Sunday when his vehicle struck James Alan Beri, 20, who was riding a bike, according to the North Dakota Highway Patrol. Beri was pronounced dead at the scene. Sherman, who was arrested following the incident, was released after posting $1,000 bail.

While doing my (OWN) research NOT that I should have to, on a public site www.ndcourts.gov, looking up defense attorney Bruce D. Quicks that represented Joshua Alan Sherman, original charges were discovered. Manslaughter Class B felony but later reduced to negligent homicide Class C Felony and Deemed as a misdemeanor in the court's eyes? Leaving the scene of an accident involving death Class B felony later Dismissed, DUI Class B misdemeanor later Dismissed. Escape Class A misdemeanor Plead guilty according to online court site suspended sentence one year. Previous conviction of criminal mischief Class C Felony filed in October 2007 dropped to A misdemeanor. No news coverage of this? How surprising, but it was over five thousand dollars in damage to the golf course in Carrington.

In the news story, it is too short to even question, therefore I will do their jobs and state what I would be asking. What was the official cause of death? Who all was involved? What was he doing on the gravel road? Like, come on! This is frustrating. How hard is it to be a news reporter and/or do their jobs? I will say I am guilty of not checking out the scene that night or the day after, but I would have never known that it was MY job to do so. What is the point of having a police force and/or a state's attorney in this town? When they don't care? They would rather see other lives being destroyed by letting him get off scot-free?

Who was this man who got killed? He was an Iraq veteran that served his country. Instead of getting killed overseas, he gets killed here in a small town living in it for less than a year. It makes me sick thinking about it; maybe it will make you feel sick too. What you are about to hear, or see may be disturbing. There was an investigation done for a wrongful death suit, not that money can heal or bring back a person, right? I heard the 911 recording in it where the suspect claims that he thinks he hit a deer not a person. Made me angry and sickened to my stomach hearing that. I was not one to look for the truth and/or question the alleged accident but throughout this story I would have too.

As I write this, it brings me back there, feeling anger, hurt, and lost as I tell this story. It won't be easy but must be told. If I would've known what I know now, I would have left Carrington before going down a road of self-destruction that made me the person I am today. Me and my family are the victims; I felt it was opposite that the guy that killed him was a victim because of the way people would represent him, claiming he felt bad for what he did, comments made like Joshua wanted to commit suicide for what he had done, but you will decide who is and/or isn't the victim as I continue to write this story.

As far as court proceedings go, trial should have not been done in Foster County. A state's attorney and/or some legal representative should have filed for a change of venue. A change of venue is the legal term for moving a trial to a new location. In high-profile matters, a change of venue may occur to move a jury trial away from a location where a fair and impartial jury may not be possible.

I believe due to the fact of it being a small community, there could have been a conflict of interest and I believe there was one. Furthermore, it could have been considered a big or important case with the parties involved. Not sure how experienced the state's attorney was as far as cases involving death go. From what I have seen, read, and heard he should have never been elected to the office. Rumors that he ran against his ex-wife was the only reason he was placed in elected office. According to a YouTube video posted. He himself admits to running against his wife and taking the bar exam four times.

I always believed in the justice system growing up thinking

it was fair and balanced how it SHOULD be, but the state's attorney and others involved would bring me to see the reality of it. If we allow them to get away with this, how are we any better? Who will hold them accountable for their suspected criminal actions and/or neglect for not preserving justice? You will see documents that claim that the defendant served one year in a southwestern correctional facility reporting on a day after my brother got killed? Strange, does this man have a time machine? Was someone sloppy with their paperwork and/or was it an intentional cover-up? Why were they gonna have him serve his time in another correctional facility in the western part of the state? Either way, big case, right? This guy took a human life and never paid for it. I WILL remind you James served his country and didn't deserve what happened to him.

Next, I will write the steps on how to use this site. If there are questions about the authenticity. After that, I will show you key information that supports the story.

Type www.ndcourts.gov.
2. Click search record and/or pay fines.
3. Click here to proceed. Click it of-coarse.
4. You can either click district for the location or Click on State of North Dakota.
5. Click criminal or traffic you can also search other areas.
6. The defendant is always marked; you can look up cases by attorneys as well. Type in his or anyone's name, then click administration traffic, then shift scroll down to select all of them if you wish.

1. NEGLIGENT HOMICIDE
Pled Guilty
Confinement:
Agency: SW Multi-County Corrections Center, Term: 0 Year, 0 Month, 365 Days Report on: July 8, 2008
Suspended: 0 Year, 0 Month, 1 Day
Credit for Time Served: 0 Year, 0 Month, 2 Days

Condition - Adult:

1. Supervised Probation, 702 SUPERVISED PROBATION, DCWHO: JAMESTOWN DISTRICT PAROLE & PROBATION 04/14/2009 - 07/08/2014, Satisfied 08/09/2012

Condition - Adult:

1. Converted Conditions, 696 DEEMED A MISDEMEANOR 04/14/2009, Active 04/14/2009

08/08/2012 **Motion Index # 20**

to Terminate Probation

08/09/2012 **Order Index # 21**

to Terminate Probation

05/31/2013 **Letter Index # 22**

letter deeming misdemeanor

Fee Totals:

Fine/State $500.00 Criminal Administration Fee $400.00 Defense/Facility Admin Fee $100.00 Fee Totals $1,000.00

04/14/2009 Plea (Judicial Officer: Judge, Conversion)

1. ESCAPE

Guilty

Confinement:

Agency: SW Multi-County Corrections Center, Term: 1 Year, 0 Month, 0 Day Suspended: 1 Year, 0 Month, 0 Day0 Year, 0 Month, 0 Day

04/14/2009 **Continuance**

(130) JURY OF TWELVE

05/15/2008 **Disposition**

1. CRIMINAL MISCHIEF

Pled Guilty

Condition - Adult:

1. Unsupervised Probation, 703 UNSUPERVISED PROBATION 05/15/2008, Active 05/15/2008 Fee Totals:

Criminal Administration Fee $200.00 Defense/Facility Admin Fee $100.00 Victim-Witness Fee $25.00 Restitution $6,360.67 Fee Totals $6,685.67

I received an email from Jonathan Aljets of Carrington, North Dakota, commenting that he should have been charged with capital murder. What he meant by that, I don't know, but it made me even more obsessed with finding out the truth no matter how deep I would have to dig. The judge in this case also mysteriously dies from a form of lung disease. Whether it was karma and/or murder made to look like natural causes, it is hard to determinate.

Few paragraphs I have found googling capital murder; whether it falls under federal investigation would be hard to know at this point. The person that made that comment recently passed away.

> "Capital murder is murder that may be punished by death. Capital murder involves murder plus some types of aggravating circumstances, such as murdering a police officer or firefighter while they are on duty, murdering a person while committing another felony like rape or abduction, or murdering a child.
>
> First-degree homicide by vehicle: This is a felony that, upon conviction, will result in a sentence of between 3 and 15 years of imprisonment (or between 5 and 20 years for habitual violators), with no parole for at least 1 year. A homicide is a first-degree homicide by vehicle if the driver "unlawfully met or overtook a school bus; unlawfully failed to stop after a collision; was driving recklessly; was driving while under the influence of alcohol or drugs; failed to stop for, or otherwise was attempting to flee from, a law enforcement officer; or had previously been declared a habitual violator."

A message was sent to me through the messenger, messagebook, and/or email. I contacted my lawyer at the time and he advised me to bring it to the court's attention but nothing happened, like they ignored it or threw it away.

> Unedited message from Joshua Alan Sherman: If your brother was as worthless fuck as you are. Im am glad the piece of shit commited suicide by riding his bike into my

pickup. Dated Aug of 13th 2011 7:37 AM

I was in shock waking up to that message. Is this still sounding like an accident? I would think this would warrant an investigation not local but state or federal.

> Jonathan Aljets
> Aug. 29, 1995 - Oct. 27, 2020
> CARRINGTON, N.D. – Jonathan Aljets, 25, Carrington, N.D., died Tuesday, Oct. 27, in his home.

The last time I saw or hung out with him was in 2016–2017. I never noticed any depression back then. Seemed like he was getting his life back together. He used to be slender, rumored that he used to smoke and/or use meth. I cannot confirm it personally, but he was involved in drug activity, according to court public information. Jonathan quit smoking, then started gaining a lot of weight fast. I must have met him through another coworker at the job. He looked like a different person, and at one point in time, we were close friends for a short period.

He was a bit crazy but in a positive way. We would have a few beers, us talking about life and my brother's case. He suggested we should talk to Marcus about his involvement in it. At the time, I was suspicious and paranoid of Marcus but took his advice. I remember him saying, "I am protected." What he meant by that, I don't know, but I can hope that protection is still in effect. At this point, I would question his death not out of disrespect for the family but because he seemed to know more about the case than he led me to believe.

Back to the point, after my brother got killed, I escalated in my drinking. Criminal activities, charges involving minors in consumption, criminal mischief aka vandalism, fleeing police, all mainly misdemeanors, but one felony on juvenile record involving terrorizing resulting in me pointing a BB gun at someone. I can't remember the circumstances surrounding it, but I was drunk and outnumbered. Officer Erickson was the one that arrested me. She had me take my shoes off because she didn't want me running from her, which I have in the past.

Shortly after my brother's life was taken from us. I would visit the location where they claimed it was taken. Erickson came out not knowing that I had a BB gun strapped in my waistline. She surprised me by giving me a hug which was odd at the time but sweet that she did care about what I was experiencing. I must have thought I was a gangsta back then. One night she picked me and a friend up for a curfew violation. She must have known I was drinking because she told me I was being dropped off last. For some reason, she had me stand in front of her police cruiser. As she knocked on the door, then turning her head. I was gone running north towards the pasta plant hiding in the fields.

Police were searching, plus another person that was friends with Erickson. Neither of them found me that night, ended up hitchhiking towards New Rockford, made it there in the afternoon, which was only fifteen miles away. I can't recall whether I was picked up or not. Erickson did come to the trailer the next day to arrest me. For some reason, this was my first time that she read the Miranda rights. I never remembered them read in any other arrests in this period. Knowing this presently, I would've fought all my charges because of my young age, lack of knowledge, and all the drinking. I never fought them. Erickson's friend, I referred to her at one point as Detective Mary Brown aka "big butt brown" is what Elmer referred to her as. Unfortunately got her tires slashed for her cooperation with the police. You can probably guess why she earned that nickname because her butt is a very noticeable part of her body. Brown later ended up working for the state's attorney as a paralegal and/or a secretary.

I am not proud of what I have done, but I didn't know how else to handle my anger and/or hurt of what I was feeling at the time. I was slowly but surely pushing everyone away from me. Before my eighteenth birthday, I got placed in the custody of DJS, which stands for Division of Juvenile Services.

Dennis was my probation officer. He then sent me to YCC Youth Correctional Center in Mandan, North Dakota, for a twenty-one-day evaluation while I was there. It was the first time I showered with other guys. I never did drop the soap because there were dispensers on the wall. Our uniforms were green and we wore sandals instead of shoes.

    I never showered during gym because I was too shy, scared and/or it was weird for me. When I was a teenager in high school, I couldn't afford to dress like other students. I would get teased and/or bullied about wearing the same clothes to school, but I didn't know any better. I was in special education, not for how I dressed but because I had a lazy mind. I don't regret growing up the way I did. I have a lot of great childhood memories. The holidays in the winter months always hit me the hardest every year emotionally except for Christmas, followed by snow, lights, and the smell of a fresh pine tree. I would go up north for a white Christmas. Hard to tell if the snow would stay on the ground. Temperatures change like crazy. What is the point of having a weatherperson anymore? How dare they tell us what kind of weather we should be having.

    Remembering laughing so hard with my roommate and/or cellmate was so bad that they had to separate us. I did enjoy the radio they turned on every night, had a good life experience, met a few good people, and watched a show called *Hogan's Heroes*. A guard thanked me for bringing it to his attention. The food wasn't too bad that I noticed and/or remembered. When outside, I always thought about running to escape; not sure how far I would have got, but it was on my mind all the time. Luckily. I didn't go through with it.

    I met a friend in there. His name was Gunnar, but he passed away this year from an accident/murder case that makes no sense. The story on that is he crashed on his motorcycle, and someone may have choked him. According to a public go fund page cause, of death was Asphyxiation. The news never did a report on it or update the public of the cause of death and/or any other details months later. There were rumors that he was an informant it would explain why he was in and out of jail so quickly.

Organizer
News tonight from officers, Gunnar did not pass due to the accident. There was no broken bones or internal bleeding. Gunnar passed away from asphyxiation. The officers stated this is an on-going investigation. They are not ruling out anything at this point. Things are not adding up and they are going to find the answers. Please keep the family in your prayers!

I would be interested in knowing what took place that day with Gunnar. It may help or be related to my brother's case in some way. The reasoning is it sounds similar to what took place in 2008. Claiming to be accidental, when in fact it may have been an intentional murder looks can be deceiving. The alleged accident may not have gone as planned. He could have still been alive but finished off by person and/or persons. Thinking capital murder may apply in James's case due to him serving his country. James may also have been a victim of Aggravated and/or Murder For Hire possible motives at this time are. He knew something became a threat to the person and/or persons involved, and/or he slept with someone's girlfriend. As state's attorney Don would say something similar, it's not what you think or know it's what you can prove.

Surprisingly YCC ruled that I was not a danger to the community. I was released back into Carrington. My memory is blurry but thinking I committed some crimes here that I can't recall. Dennis then placed me in an inpatient treatment center called Center For Solutions in Cando, North Dakota. Before we move forward, I would like to make a note. I did not know how much stress and frustration I was putting my parents through until after the fact, but they refused to give up on me and kept trying to stray me in the right direction. On another note, Elmer mentioned I could have sued Joshua for either wrongful death suit and/or because he was responsible for me being in treatment. He would say that Joshua killed my brother, not the insurance company.

Welcome to Center for Solutions. My first time in a treatment facility was a well-run facility. While in treatment, I turned eighteen, never smoked before but I got a cigar on my birthday when I started the nasty habit. The only other time I remember touching cigarettes was when James and I were on a bridge in New Rockford lighting fireworks off with them. The guy that gave me the grape cigar would later work here. I don't remember how and why he got the job. Unfortunately, the group that I was in the clients made up of the opposite sex. The counselors were also both female. How was I able to relate to anything or anyone?

One counselor had a pair of brass balls that symbolizes courage. She would have clients wear them and a bullshit button, always claiming clients would be blowing smoke up her ass. What did she mean by that, maybe someone kissing her ass? Every time it came to me sharing, I'd lock down my mind. Thinking it was because I was refusing to feel or process my emotions and/or realize the truth of what allegedly happened that night. For the first time another client and I made hooch. We had it hidden under the pool table. He started telling others about it. I warned him, but he continued, and both of us got busted for it. Thinking both of us are going to get kicked but I remained there but had my bags packed just in case.

I've run away from the treatment center several times and not knowing where I was going, but knew I didn't want to be there mentally. When a cop located, then placed me in his car, I should have told him a joke that he was going the wrong way. The jail is in the opposite direction. The center took me back several times when they had the chance to send me to county jail. Remembering I was easy to identify for some reason always buzzed my hair, felt the relief of stress, and/or reminded me not to forget my brother.

While here I got on medication, none of it was the kind you could abuse though pills were for anxiety, depression,

A HUMAN, THEN A BUILDING, NOW A RISING STOCK

and sleep. These pills would later be referred to as skittles while I stayed in MCC Chicago. I would have trouble breathing outside. I don't think I needed pills but took them as an easy way of dealing with it? We were able to have cell phones but remained in the locked office, which got broken into at one time.

I remember a guy fingering a chick right in the upstairs day room. I also learned how to play a card game called rummy. Some other activities included bowling and going to a building to play volleyball. There was a girl in there. She had a crush on me. Whether she liked me or hoped to use me for something, maybe picking half-smoked cigarettes out of the outside ashtrays.

Why this place cared so much is what I was thinking at the time. For some reason, they took an attentive interest in me because they knew they could help or the fact I lost a brother. I went through the program successfully, they claimed. Thinking okay, he's better now? I came out worse. It could have been that I was refusing to talk about what was bothering me. They also could have poked the bear (ME) and/or rattled the black box? Either way, it was a waste of time and money, but I was released and enrolled into a youth-works program in Bismarck, North Dakota, where I received my first lap dance while staying in their housing.

Well, you'd be wrong thinking I followed the program. I started drinking again and abusing Robitussin, which is a cough syrup in pill form that contained a chemical in there that would get you high or make you hallucinate. I was not buying it nor did I buy the booze I was drinking, wristwatch, DVDs, knives, and other items I ended up obtaining without cash or card. I never was once charged with theft but did face a charge of hit and run—why I didn't report this you can probably guess why. I don't remember if I bought a stereo or stole it cause of the size but do remember stacking DVDs in my jacket then taking them to the bathroom where I would pry open the case with a knife then taking the disc out stashing the rest in the trash can. If they were to think about it, this idea I got would save them a lot of money. Another time I surprisingly didn't get caught at another store. I would jack knives by seeing the security strip, then cutting it out and stashing knifes in my jacket and/or pants legs.

As I was walking out, they were slipping out of my pant leg. Another time I stole a watch, thought I disabled the security, but as I walked out, it went off, and to avoid attention, I just kept walking normal, then running once I got far enough away. Anyways, at this point in the story, I ended up leaving youth works moving in with a cougar woman that I was sleeping with, meeting her through a friend I meant at the homeless shelter. I remember her saying don't take that stuff (Robitussin) is what she was referring to cause I couldn't perform well with it in my system. She would joke around saying get it up or get out but felt somewhat at home cause I was in a trailer park. When I left her, I promised I would be back but never returned. Remembering I didn't like kissing her because lips were too slippery was a weird feeling. She did let me drive her car. That was cool, I guess. One night, getting beer from a store, the cashier yelled, "What the hell you think you're doing?" Guys I was hanging out with drove up front picking me up. Another time I went into this dark-lighted liquor store was able to walk out with a few half-gallons of whiskey unnoticed and/or detected.

It feels good thinking back on it, however, if caught more fines and change of past. I am questioning whether I felt bad about it or not. That is just the dark side talking. While I was living there meant several people, one individual claimed he was in a gang called shotgun cripes was it real or not? The requirement to join was to stand and take a beat down for five minutes, and of course, I did this now a shotgun crip part of a family, I thought anyways. If true or not, I always was high or drunk eventually felt like the guy's little b***h at one point, not a respected gang member. One day we went somewhere and, I ditched him ran to a hotel to tell the desk clerk I had warrants so she would call the police. It turned out that Dennis withdrew active warrants because my brother was going to pick me up to take me back to Carrington then treatment. I don't remember agreeing to this arrangement. If the police responded, it could have been a different story, which reminds me to backtrack.

What set me up to fail at the start, I had to stay in a homeless shelter called Ruth Meiers Hospitality House. for a length of time before entering into the youth works program, which was scary for me. At the time, I tossed my coin on the ground that I received from treatment. Thinking they failed me because I have never been in a homeless shelter, nor did I know anyone except this one guy. I meant in Carrington once while having car trouble. Thinking at this point, I went to the homeless shelter for food pantry items and/or something else. Dennis put out an APB for my arrest. An all-points bulletin (APB) is a broadcast issued from any American or Canadian law enforcement agency to its personnel, or to other law enforcement agencies. It typically contains information about a wanted suspect who is to be arrested or a person of interest, for whom law enforcement officers are to look.

I ended up changing my jacket at the shelter because the police were circling, and they were looking for me but never were able to locate me. Anyways at the hotel, I had to ditch my Robitussin and a few knives I had on my person. I then ended up sleeping in the hotel lobby. Eventually, my brother did pick me up in a red Ford pickup F-150. I ended up spending a few days with family and friends, drinking of-course, before going back to treatment in Cando. As I didn't mention the first time, they pat you down and go through your bags for drugs and alcohol. Which I believe was a good idea, but others hiding items may disagree. The staff was friendly. I miss the place, why wouldn't I? It's what changed me and helped me on a course to a better direction for myself and others.

This one cook named Kelly would always make my favorite hot-dish, which was tater tot hot-dish or casserole. Another staff member had a good sense of humor that made the stay more enjoyable. Another staff member who had blonde hair giggled a lot. He could have been a corrections/police officer or something along those lines. I give that place a lot of credit for turning my life around. The second group I was in had mixed-sex. I was able to make more progress even the counselors were one female and one male. They may have changed this because them knowing that I was not successful the first time in a group of mostly women who will know the answers? Anyway, something happened when it was my turn to talk. I would shut down and run away again. One day I agreed to do an individual session with Ben, but in return, he told me about his past as a biker and what he experienced.

I ran his name through the site www.bop.gov to confirm he was telling the truth. Somehow his story got me to open up for the first time, tears shooting out of my eyes, blowing my nose with a box of Kleenex. The second time I broke down since losing my brother keeping all that hate, hurt, and anger in wasn't nor is still healthy for me and any other human bean, but this was a turning point for both of us. I told him I didn't see myself being completely sober for the rest of my life. He then replied, can you at least get to the point of cutting down and/or controlling it. To this day, I can stop at drinking one beer instead of having one after another.

I remember I was set in my ways, unwilling to change that no one was going to change me for the better. I was angry at the world heading down a dark path, but one session with Ben impacted the course of my life forever. To this day, I still have hurt that needs to be processed but scared to do it alone reasoning is my emotions are deep and hard to control if processed in large amounts will further explain in the story. Ben earned my trust because of his back-round troubles with law enforcement. To my understanding, he came into the profession to help others like him and me with similar difficulties and/or losses. To this day, I would highly recommend him to anyone, but the only catch is you would have to be willing to change yourself before accepting any help from others for it to be fully effective.

Back then, I didn't care, but he and other key people and events in my life helped me become the person I am today. Ben would claim I am still in recovery; can't argue with his opinion on it.

Through the lost dazed and confusion
According to www.ndcourts.gov, I was still in Carrington after being released from treatment. Around this period, I gained employment as a cashier at Stop-In-Go, where I positively identified the guy that killed my brother for the first time. Joshua came in multiple times using his credit or debit card. Naturally, I got curious and found out who he was by looking at the name on a signature slip. I am confident enough to state that Joshua knew who I was, and aware of his actions and intentions, what he was doing. But why would he be doing this to me? I felt like his intention towards me was to intimidate me, brag, and/or show off, what Joshua had done to my family and me. He should have been in JAIL and, or there should have at least been a no-contact order in a place like what is wrong or going on here?

I talked to the manager she said she couldn't do anything about it, claiming they brought in a lot of money and business. I surprisingly was able to wait on him but didn't have much to say awkwardly, got quiet, shaky, and avoided eye contact with him. I remember one visit so well where I recall one item he bought, which was called Gas-X. Jean miler, a co-worker at the time, offered to wait on him. I thought about the saying, what doesn't kill you will make you stronger. I declined the offer. A person would later say I must be a beast by now with everything I went through in life. I'd always joke with customers saying they should wait till they leave the store before drinking their monster energy drink.

I first meant Mrs. Miller while attending high school in New Rockford. She was a substitute teacher there. I would always joke with her in school and was considered the class clown. I would play dumb, but she would always take me seriously. I will never forget her. She recently passed away.

After my encounter with Joshua, I eventually started to target people that deserved my justice how I looked at it back then by slashing three tires. I helped a friend out with her problems involving an ex of hers, resulting in more slashed tires. I believe the statute of limitations has expired at this time just as a caution. I'll leave specific details out. Her name was Bonnie. At the time, I didn't feel like she used and/or took advantage of my skills until after I retired or slowed down from my criminal activities involving tires. We didn't hang out as much, nor was she there to help me out. Slashing tires wasn't only a way to relieve my hate, anger, and revenge but also came with an adrenaline rush. I remember cops knocking on Bonnie's door several times. The police were looking for me or my shoes. The reason for shoes was to match them up for imprints left at the scene of a crime. While at Bonnie's, I would hide my shoes. After the police left empty-handed, we would make fun of and laugh at them.

Remembering Elmer mentioning I should have just let the air out of the tires would have taken longer avoided charges but would have taken job security away from the local tire shops. The police would have been bored. Victims would have looked foolish. Yes, Joshua was one target. I may have slashed four of his tires in one night. I got charged for damage relating to Joshua. I can't recall if it was cause they assumed, branded, and/or my friend snitched on me. What I mean, by branded, once I was caught slashing one tire. The police, state's attorney, and the general public thought I was responsible for every tire slashed in Carrington. Elmer did agree to testify against me.

When I was staying over at Marcus's, I went out to randomly slash tires. A guy from the party followed me, then detained me, and called the police. He weighed a lot because I couldn't get away from him, but I have not forgotten his name to this day. After that, I am sure they had me marked as a confirmed suspect. I cannot recall how many tires I was responsible for slashing or other damage done in Carrington. The state attorney's window got smashed around this time. He would say to my lawyer I know Billy did it, but I can't prove it. He still alleges I did it to this day.

At this time, I must have been in between jobs getting drunk every day, and committing crimes. The last charges filed and dismissed on me for this period was April 5th, 2010. sometime after this, I moved out of the city and into Gladstone. I was hoping to use tracebook to track it, but www.ndcourts.gov tracks my location because of the guy that stole my Xbox. I was able to look up his name and, the filing date for his charge was 09/29/2010. The arrival date for Gladstone would be spring or summer of 2010. 2011 is where one lostbook account tracked some events of my life. To my best ability will explain what took place here. Gladstone, North Dakota, western side of state about 10 miles from Dickinson with my dog Ladybird formally named Jimmy after my brother but changed it because of my father's disapproval for the name. Remembering him saying something like the dead should be left alone, I believe shortly after losing my brother, I got her or in 2009.

My brother Alex ended up finding her running around in the streets of Devils Lake, North Dakota, Alex wanted to adopt her, but due to him living in a group home, he was not allowed to keep her. So, I ended up adopting her from the animal shelter where she had to stay for some time to see if her owners would claim her. I picked her up for the first time in my greyish Ford Taurus, which I cannot remember who I bought the car from, but Ladybird was shaky and scared would want to sit in my lap or crawl around my neck while driving. I got the idea to name her Ladybird from the show king of the hill.

Welcome to Gladstone. My parents brought a trailer-house there eventually moved it into the city of Carrington, later on in this story. Parents influenced me to move there because it be far enough away and, out of Carrington, this would be considered a fresh start for me. Here I am, filled with excitement to get out of town but missing my family, friends and, more challenges would arise. One big challenge was living without running water for nine months. The plan to install new water lines inside the trailer house project would prove to be easy because of the experience I had obtained involving PEX water lines, but I can't recall if that was after or before the move to Gladstone.

Parents that won the wrongful death suit used the money to invest in the trailer house business, which you also will find out more about as time goes on. If, I would have known the future. I would have talked my parents into keeping the money and moving out of the area. Unfortunately, I was not around to voice any option if I had one at the time. I was still struggling to deal with a loss. I learned that the guy that killed my brother was walking free, never helped matters. I never wanted to be in the handyman trailer park business but was forced into it in a way because of my parents. I couldn't just bail on them. The option was there, but I never took it.

Anyway, with this trailer house, there was a water hookup to it, but the city would make claims and/or excuses to deny me water. During this time, the oil boom was happening, which I am confident of this playing a role in it. One of the many excuses the city used was an unpaid water bill. Parents paid it, still no water. I can't recall all of them, but it would explain why the previous owner sold it. I am thinking, neither of my parents had any knowledge of it. Not another ambush? Parents owned the trailer house and three additional lots, which later were lost and sold to the city due to unpaid back taxes. My mom attempted to sell the land. The city blocked the sale claiming there was a lien on it. Things were not adding up, nor is there any explanation for it. We did work on getting lawyers on board to sue the city, but it never happened. My best guess is we didn't have enough money and/or the lawyers didn't want to get involved, for some reason.

When we first came here, which included me, my brother, and my mother. If I remember correctly, my brother Cookie only stayed for a bit and took back off to Carrington. First person or couple we met was this guy named Jose and his girlfriend Chelsey, giving us a friendly welcome.

Jose would later end up stealing my Xbox 360. At one time, we were roommates, but he was running behind on rent, and/or other issues came up resulting in me kicking him out. One day while I was at work, Jose came into the trailer house through a window and/or him still having a key to the door. Jose took my Xbox and pawned it, which is the only reason he got caught for it. Luckily, I taped a sticker on the back of the hard drive from my medication I used to take, which is how police were able to identify it as my property.

Speaking of police, there were many times I wouldn't answer my door because even though I was out of Carrington. The state's attorney would still file charges against my person, unsure if he had proof to back them up or not. I suspected him of trying to get a rise out of me, scare me into pleading guilty, and some a type of intimation. He did have a grudge against me because his office door window got shattered. I never was charged, but our family lawyer told my dad that Don claimed that he knew I done it but couldn't prove it. The last time I saw him at the courthouse was in 2018. He still brought it up, asking for me to admit to it. Every time Don issued warrants for my arrest, police came at night knocking on my door in return, I hid behind the couch and waited for them to leave.

Also, I couldn't talk with them because of my drinking. One night when I answered the door, they were looking for Jose. I made the mistake of allowing them to search for him in return for my cooperation. I got charged with underage drinking. The police went as far as taking the empty bottles with a drop of liquor in them as evidence. I never went to jail that night but did later down the road when I didn't pay my fines. I went into the trailer for about fifteen minutes. I came back out and, there was a cop waiting for me. How strange? Did someone call or give them a heads up? Why was a warrant for unpaid fines related to a minor in possession urgent to them? I couldn't say anything awful about the jail. If I remember right, it had carpet and windows. Maybe this is why Joshua wanted to serve his time here?

Eventually, I meant more people in Gladstone, gaining employment at the scrap yard. I enjoyed being around all of my coworkers. I was a shop assistant working with another person whose name was Jerry, soon to be a buyer for my liquor. We took in all the small metals, weighing them and writing the tickets. When things slowed down, we would run the can crusher. A conveyor belt would carry, then drop the cans where a car tire would crush them and blow them into a trailer. If I ever came into work hungover and/or drunk from the night before, he would know and make me pay for it by working my butt off, therefore sweating it out. I didn't mind it, started to enjoy it after a while, and it became part of my improved work ethic throughout life.

I had a good job, girlfriend, and friends only if I had that water would have been perfect. I was only making $9.00 an hour at the time, but it was worth it because of the coworkers. I learned how to operate a forklift then the payloader. I would only move it in and out of the shop and, I wanted to know more eventually. Thinking high point of living in Gladstone was the Summer of 2010 when I rose then eventually would fall and thought I had it all. Around this time, I met Megan through a mutual friend. We would hang out and play drinking games, one game called riding the bus if I remember right. She was the farmer's daughter and, we connected in some way.

I remember taking somewhat of a shower in the lake by her farm. She was the one that asked if we were a couple, both of us being shy. Of course, I replied with a confirmed yes. I am not sure how long it lasted. She was a virgin, didn't wanna have sex tell marriage. I do consider it one of the best relationships I have had in life. I believe the reason we broke up was because of my behavior at the time. Even though I went through treatment, I was still working on cleaning up my act and, I believe her sister influenced the breakup. I never did get a good reason as to why she ended it with me.

Later in writing, I'd rise higher in 2017. I remember I had this gray cat named hustler. You can guess or use your imagination as to why I picked that name. He was a good cat. A friend named Lester gave me the cat. Lester will end up coming into the story when I return to Carrington. The cat got sick. I then took him to the vet, where a veterinarian injected something into him, maybe to hydrate him? He ended up urinating all over the floor. After the visit, I took him home and was out of town for a few days, but during my absence, my roommates were supposed to keep an eye on him. When I returned home, he was dead, guessing he may have gotten into some poison or neglected while I was absent. Don't worry. I never threw him in the trash. I gave him a proper burial with rocks on top so dogs couldn't dig him up.

Eventually, I met another friend. They called him PJ meeting him in the same time frame. He would always come over to drink with me and keep me company, thinking it was cause he felt sorry for me. Presently we keep in contact by email but no calling or hanging out. I never will go near or in North Dakota unless I had no choice. I contacted PJ asking him to help me out with this, but he never showed any interest. It sucks to be alone if I wasn't. I wouldn't be where I am today. I used to beg for other's attention but not anymore.

While living in the trailer house, with everything turned on except the water. During the late fall, I chased most of my friends away then it was just my dog and me. Eventually, a friend did move in. Yes, I was still drinking every day, did you need to ask? Luckily, the job I had was working at a scrap yard, so I never had to shower every day at a truck stop. I did the best I could with what I had. At one point, I was getting water from the apartments to flush toilets until the manager put a stop to it. After that, I had to urinate outside and place a plastic bag inside the toilet bowl for solid waste. I should have just built an outhouse, but I never thought clearly about it; wouldn't have been a bad idea at the time.

I lived like this for about nine months. It was depressingly lonely. I started branding or burning myself with a spiral from a notebook and got the scars to prove it. The last time I did this was after a short breakup in 2017. I am thinking I did this for multiple reasons, one, releasing pain I was feeling, and two, asking for help in a way. Three, showing how much pain I was going through and/or a form of self-discipline.

Jerry and I would always talk about how sickening life was. There would be a blizzard outside and, a person would think it would be a slow day. Unfortunately, people still came in during blizzards and/or winter storms. If it was just one battery, a pound of cans, or a radiator, they came in. We had to be careful with handling batteries due to the acid in them if leaked out. The acid would put holes in your clothes. Jerry was not only a good coworker but a friend as well. We bonded well and felt like a family working here. Jerry was not only a good coworker but a friend as well. We got along well and felt like a family working here.

One night, I was drinking, reviewing legal paperwork involving Joshua Alan Sherman (the guy that killed my brother) with his cell phone number on it. I cannot remember if there was a good reason for it except to entrap me into calling him up like a setup. There was no reason for this. I was still mad at the guy, of course, so thinking I was texting him then at one point called. I cannot remember the whole conversation, but I do remember I felt good after I got off the phone with him and, to my knowledge, I made no threats to his life.

The next few days went by then there was a temporary restraining order put in place and a charge of terrorizing against my person. Joshua, along with a police officer, claiming to be a witness to the phone call. Further claiming, I threatened to slit his throat. I don't believe it went like that if I remember clearly. I asked him questions about the alleged accident. He was claiming he was turning his life around by giving drunk driving speeches to schools.

So what was a cop doing there if there was one that even existed? Why would this guy feel threatened by me? Thinking it was because I slashed his tires, which I got charged for in November. He may have been thinking, I knew something about the accident and/or wanting to discredit me for good? I get more talkative while drinking. I have never been one to express what I felt, nor would I voice threats out loud. All my anger was action carried out by slashing tires. Let's say this did go down as they claim. Who in my shoes wouldn't want to get revenge or be upset with this guy? The state's attorney put his phone number on my paperwork could he have been that dumb and/or was he acting like it? Carrington is three hours away; it would have made more sense to voice that threat while in Carrington.

I am afraid this wouldn't be the first time later on in the story Joshua would claim I was stalking him in Carrington. While I was getting gravel to level a mobile home that moved from Gladstone, the same one I lived in without running water. Joshua filed a police report claiming I was following him and there was a restraining order in effect. I got gravel from a shop to put underneath the trailer, then twenty minutes later, a deputy and a city officer showed up. I was shaking, explaining to them that I never was in contact with him, then was arrested and booked in the county jail. Later on, I read the officer's report that looked to me like it was just the opposite that he was stocking and/or following me. The event occurred on or about the date of 8/20/2011 charge was eventually dismissed.

So, during this time, I was still working at the scrapyard, my boss Clay and family lawyer were keeping in close contact with each other. I don't recall why I gave permission and allowed it at the time. Eeryone was thinking I'd be in jail for a few months. I had all my affairs taken care of. I then drove east on 94 towards Carrington to turn myself into the jail, somewhere between Gladstone and Bismarck. I hit a slick spot and rolled the car. I can't remember it because it happened so fast, but I was glad I didn't have my dog with me. I never got a scratch and my second rollover.

My first one happened the same way also walked away with no scratches. Thinking I braced for impact by putting my hands against the roof when it rolled. For some reason, the state patrol had my phone number, called, and asked if I knew I had a warrant out. I explained to him the plan the officer either understood or probably was wondering what I was smoking, like who turns themselves in? When my mom picked me up, the game plan was to turn myself into Carrington, but that changed, and we went straight to the county jail in Devils Lake. At the time, Carrington mainly used this jail to hold inmates when Jamestown was only 40 miles away.

When we arrived, my mom asked if I wanted a subway sandwich, I replied no. Who would have an appetite after rolling their car and now turning themselves into jail? I then hugged my mom and went inside the big steel door. The case opened on January 11, 2011 case lasted until or was closed on 02-12-12. There was a bond set and posted maybe, rolling my car and turning myself in paid off? Who knows, I was back in the Gladstone area where a coworker sold me a Mazda. A good pickup only had to replace a battery, belt, and something else.

I don't recall any key events happening until the spring of 2011 didn't wanna be in Gladstone anymore. I wanted to be back in Carrington parents would argue against it. I never asked or went back. I contacted a friend whose dad was living in Sheyenne, decided to give that a try. I was only there for a few days or weeks, then returning. The reason why is it was too quiet and/or boring there. I would have had to adjust to the area, which is always a struggle for me. My thought is with silence. I am alone with myself, which I would have had to face my emotions. One must eventually sit down with himself or herself and face the problems head-on. We all can run but can't hide forever, especially from ourselves.

Welcome back to Gladstone not sure what I was doing besides drinking here. Eventually, there was a plan set in place to move the trailer house to Carrington. It was my responsibility to oversee and prepare the trailer house for transport, the assistance provided by my coworkers. My tracebook account comes into play on February 4th, 2011. I did state I was planning on moving back. I was frustrated around this time because the police were looking for a fugitive named Jose Garza. The same guy that stole my Xbox not sure how many days this was going on, maybe a week according to my tracebook status updates.

I am thinking, during the Spring/Summer, I turned in all my metals I had saved up during this time. There were a lot of beer cans, of course, other small metals and copper. Ain't sure if PJ was around to help me or not. He may have been living in Dickinson. I will be given credit to my coworkers at Continental metals, General Scrap, and Evraz. Its current name Roberson Metal Recycling. At the time, the company went under three different names. Knowledge is power comes into play here. Evraz was the parent owner, which is a Russian-owned company. General Scrap name covered scrap yards in Dickinson, Minot, and/or other cities. Continental metals were the name of the one scrap yard in Dickinson's location.

The reasoning for this might have been to hide who owned the company, which were Russians at the time. I am sure people wouldn't have supported this if they knew the truth about it. I did research when and why it changed ownership but have not found any news stories on it. Whether they reported on it and/or news article dropped off from google for whatever reason, your guess is just as good as mine. I don't know why they disclosed that information to us employees at the time. The companies may not trust their employees with too much information anymore unless it's on a need-to-know basis. As time goes on, we all get wiser if we choose to accept it and/or acknowledge it. Police are behind the criminals learning from them as the student learning from the teacher. If cops were former criminals, would they perform better? Have a better understanding of both sides of the law or a person?

Anyway, back on point here with prepping any trailer house to be moved, remove skirting around it, disconnect everything attached to it. The primary purpose of skirting trailers is to keep them insulated and animals out. Then would have to jack it up to put all the tires on which were missing. I had to take multiple trips back and forth to Carrington to obtain what was needed like, tires, bricks, and a trailer jack. There was a deck on the front of it that needed to be detached. Easier said than done. I attempted to move it with my pickup, apparently wasn't thinking straight at the time or being smart. If I remember right, a coworker brought a chainsaw to cut it into salvageable pieces and later move them. (As I write, it's taking myself back emotionally, feeling that I am back there in Gladstone in my mind). I can't recall how long this took, but slowly and surely it was ready to be transported.

I offered to buy my coworkers' a taco pizza from Cowboy Pizza to show my appreciation for their help and support. When I thought I was alone there, I wasn't. They were always there for me eight hours per day, five days a week during regular business hours. I am sure if I needed them during off-work hours, they would have come through for me. When it was time to leave, I didn't have many people to say goodbye to except them. All my friends I was hanging out with left me a while ago because they didn't want to be around me with all my drinking. I drank for the wrong reasons, which has never benefited me that I know off. Drinking never made me a better person to be around.

One truebook comment my ex left on a post. I was always freaking out for no reason back then. One example of my behavior was I got a rose from Jamestown. It was for her, but I got jealous or frustrated that she wasn't responding fast enough to my texts and/or calls, taking and breaking the vase on the road. I thought my dog was an attention hoarder, but here I am, demanding it similarly.

As I looked back on my monsterbook messages in 2011, I was a negative person that no one wanted to be around. I am a prime example of how much losing a brother can affect a person's personality or life. People say just be yourself. I don't know who I am anymore or what kind of person I am. I do know I am no longer a monster and/or an animal that I used to be. My ex-girlfriend, the one that got away or I chased away, is now married with kids. I'd reach out to her, but it would be somewhat painful reliving it and, she probably wouldn't remember it or reply. I wouldn't blame anyone that gave up on me. It took me a long time to move on from her. I was attached to her emotionally and physically. It could have been a Joe Dirt and Brandy relationship if I played my cards right. I am currently single and plan on staying that way. I have heard that I am complicated couldn't argue with that, but it has its pros and cons like everything else in life.

    A person cannot change the past but can learn from it and improve their present or future. I asked for answers from the past and, Big D asked me why. I replied, bringing up the past helps to learn from it. It also gives a person the chance to process raw emotions that were suppressed by addictions. In turn, it makes one stronger. Examples: coffee beans you grind them long enough more processed they would become as swallowing whole foods would be difficult for the stomach to process. Whether it makes sense to you or not? Grinding the past into fine powder would be easier to process. People to this day would not believe how much I have changed for the better. I have hit many rock-bottoms, so many I can't count and/or keep track of them all. After losing my dog Ladybird, which devastated me the hardest for some reason, and ended up leaving North Dakota for good in 2018.

    Here I am back in Carrington when the trailer arrived assistant manager of the trailer court and others helped me set it up, stabilizing it in place. At this point, my parents had bought several trailer houses I was held responsible for the upkeep of them all. It was challenging and a new learning experience for me as the soon-to-be known Ladybirds dog house. Ladybird's dog house, named in her remembrance, got remodeled with new floors, paint, carpet, and new plumbing. When the natural gas line got tested for leaks, neither a professional from the gas company and the plumber located the leak. They both went out for lunch. I took a spray bottle filled with soap and water mixed, then sprayed outside lines by the meter, discovering the gas leak. Whether this was just luck or, maybe they weren't thinking straight.

There was a lot of money invested in the trailer house. The current owners living in it are my sister and her estranged boyfriend while working on mobile homes in-between that I was still drinking. I also started playing my online war game, hanging out with friends if I had anymore. What is this guy doing? He should have plenty of work to occupy him.

Jim was a childhood friend. We were friends for a long time but eventually burned that bridge many times. He was considered a best friend and a positive influence in my life. I never was positive back then. I always fed into a lot of negativity and always felt like I couldn't get out of a hole. It was hard to change my overall outlook and/or to accept the positive in my life. I regret a lot of my past. He was one to never give up on me. Jim was always there when needed but never took advantage of it. When he wanted to hang out, I just wanted to be selfish and avoid him drinking my life away. Moving out of New Rockford to Carrington was the biggest mistake that changed lives forever. It was like flipping a light switch.

I always was focused on being isolated, distracted, and/or drowning myself in a bottle back then. I believe there are two sides of me the dark negative past and the light positive future. Both sides fighting each other, but the good side of me is winning. It sounds crazy I know. For my kind of thinking, they may put me in the nuthouse but there are methods to my madness. Eventually, there will be a balance established that is currently missing at this time. It is hard to determine where it is and/or how to balance my person and/or mind. After my session of introspection, and through the lost, dazed, and confused AGAIN. Where to start here but going off makeabook posts and criminal track record from www.ndcourts.gov. In May of 2011, I still held anger and frustration against Joshua and the state's attorney. In or before May, there was a mediation set up between us.

Our lawyers represented us in Grand Forks, North Dakota. I overslept and was running late to get there. My dad told me to take his red ford pickup for some reason, maybe it was faster getting there? I called my lawyer gave him a heads up. Once I got there, Joshua had taken off. The family lawyer told me Joshua wanted me to pay for his lawyer. Joshua, claiming it was my fault. Wow, he couldn't wait? He expected me to pay for his lawyer HOW DARE HE. Does this sound like someone that wanted to talk issues out in hopes of settling our differences aside? This never sat well with me just made things worse throughout the story. Like I could afford his lawyer? Nor would I pay for it. There are historybook posts that I made expressing my anger and frustration back then, but they won't be included due to the language used. REVISIT?

> Unedited message from Joshua Alan Sherman. (If your brother was as worthless fuck as you are. Im am glad the piece of shit commited suicide by riding his bike into my pickup.) Dated Aug of 13th 2011 7:37 AM.

Does this still sound like an accident?

I included this message at the beginning of my writing. It somehow fits in this time frame and gives a better understanding and/or idea, a reminder of what I was struggling with at the time. I can't recall if I did anything to provoke him into sending me this message. At the time, I was glad to have what I thought would be a break in the case. On the advice of the family lawyer, I filed a restraining against Joshua. The judge, courts, and/or the State Of North Dakota threw it out quickly without considering it. I am confident this message will come in use hopefully in the future.

In my appearance for a bond hearing, the state's attorney's requested a ten thousand cash bond for my release, not ten percent of it involving the violation of the restraining order. Why so high? I can only guess that they wanted to keep me in jail, or he was thinking of the wrong case. I mentioned the charge earlier, which did occur in this period. I was living at home with my parents. Ladybird had sprained her leg.

Bonnie's kids were playing too rough with her at the double-wide trailer, the one rumored of Joshua running to after he took my brother's life. There was a new store manager for Alco, then Shopko, and now Dollar Tree. She moved into the trailer next door that my parents sold her. She is German and ended up helping me fix a cast for Ladybird's leg can't recall if I took her to the vet or not, but she did recover from it.

To be clear, I was talking about my dog, not the German lady. Ute was her name. She helped me a lot this year, providing me with a job and kept me company as a friend. Not in contact with her to this day. She would say: I swear we are our own worst enemy. Am sure it was about the employees at the time, but if you think deep into it, it could also apply in general.

Below is a lost and now recovered message that I forgot about until I searched through my old Darkbook account. In hopes of triggering my memory during this year. I do not know this person or their interest and their connection with Joshua. She may have been one of my victims during my tire slashing or my brick-throwing days. I would have to relive all of 2011 to find out. At this time, I do not plan on doing that. I never responded, not sure why. I never shared it on Darkbook either for some reason. I don't know what all I was doing this year, but I managed to get a few rises out of people. REVISIT?

> **Anonymous**: The guy that "killed your bro" didn't errase facebook, he probably blocked you. If money was worthless, again you would still be sitting down in the Jamestown Jail. If you add up all the things you have been charged for, and the things yo...u have you have to be charged for... I'm guessing it would be alot longer than 5 years, which is one of the max sentances for "murder" ... So why dont you use some correct grammer and punctuation. Educate yourself thoroughly on the justice system. Then, Then maybe some people would stand behind you.
>
> **A:** do you feel that true justice would be that he just sit in jail for life withought parole? What difference would

that make? How many days in jail have you sat for your corrupt doings throught your life time? You think money bought him out? ... Well, funny people can wipe their asses with the justice system according to you ... mhh when you were in trouble, what did you do? Oh, did your parents give the justice systmen $1,000 to bail you out of jail ... HYPOCRIT

A: All your court record shows if someone would actually take the time to look would be that you are a delinquent that obviously believes their is no authority to you? Does that come from the way you were raised? I would assume so, no one taught you how to become a saiin member of society. But, as Murphy would state, he is trying to "reform" you. But, for years, all you have been is a hoodlum.

A: I will personally give you the $350 so someone greater than yourself can tell you, that your views are the ones that are corrupt

A: As you read her police statement, im sure you need to be honest while posting there was no mention of Josh anywhere on their. It was strictkly and clearly stated that you pulled out of the trailor park, and tailgated down main street. When... you then took a right turn on 9th avenue and drove infront of their home. Where you are not to come within 100 yards because he has a disorderly conduct order against you because in December you drunkenly called him from the phone number you apparently got off of court papers. After you had over an hour phone conversation making peace with him, he didn't answer once and you leave a voicemail telling him you are going to stab him in the throat on January 1st? Or the first voicemail you left telling him to put a shotgun down his throat?? Or how about on January 1st when you contacted him breaking the restrainig order, asking to revoke your bond? or, how you were going to come in front of his house and start yourself on fire?? Why do you fail to mention any of this??

A: No one got away with anything, the judical court decided on a verdict, and you need to learn to be okay with the outcome of this, because you clearly not change the outcome. Time was served, consequences have been implimented. What consequences do you have with your behaviors

A: it got tossed because a disorderly conducrt order is when you feel a threat from someone or they will cause harm to you or your property. Obviously him, stating how he truely feels to you is neither of those situations. Even though you parade around all of his behaviors, and you fail to mention your wrong doings and actions. You don't forsea yourself being charged, when their is evidence? Especially when you put your bilegerant comments all over a blog?? I would assume that would make you look guilty to something you feel guilty about doing? Money has nothing to do with it. You feel he bought freedom? Well, money doesn't purchase the justices systems decission on what his outcome and sentence was. Maybe, you should work on your government education, so when you speak it is educational facts.

A: Living over a year without privelages? Is that free??? You sure didn't want to sit in treatment in leau of jail now did you? Why, because you would loose your privelages and freedomes as well

I never had a chance to respond nine years ago but wrote what my response would be now. Who are you? What is your interest? As for educating myself on the justice system. What would you recommend? College? People standing behind me back then... like that would happen sober or drunk. Yes, justice would have been him spending the rest of his life behind bars. What examples are the court setting for others? Like letting him walk? Is it okay to kill people? Where are the law and/order? How is this justice? I am corrupt, okay? How am I corrupt, was I elected to some kind of office that I don't know of? Yeah, I was bailed out for a thousand dollars but didn't kill someone for it. How was this so-called state's attorney trying to reform me? All my years, I have been a hoodlum. I wonder why. The guy that took my brother's life was walking around like it never happened. Three hundred fifty dollars for what?

I can back up my views of corruption and have, so it was her police statement, why was she stalking me? Pulled out of the trailer park where I lived? Was I supposed to stay there and not leave? Did his girlfriend live in the trailer park too? Wouldn't she say several voicemails? I can claim the one telling him to kill himself, but the other two have been fabricated, stabbing in the throat, someone got that idea from me slashing tires. Setting myself on fire in front of his house isn't it true Joshua is a firefighter, which would explain where that one came from. Money did not influence him getting off? Time to wake up lady. If someone was gonna accept responsibility for what they did. Why would he hire a powerhouse attorney? Why would he come into my workplace every day bragging about what he did? What I mean by bragging is him coming in sliding his card like he wanted me to know who he is and what he had done.

At the end of 2011, I started following a collective group called Anonymous them claiming to have no leadership. I can't recall how I came across them, but it was a hope that I needed at the time. For those that aren't familiar with Anonymous. It's a group that is involved in targeting the financial sector, like wall street. At the time, Anonymous may have been involved with politics myself as a collective member. I took to the streets sometime in the spring to peacefully protest, thinking it was after my dad passed away in March 2012. The motivation to protest was the injustice I received involving my brother's death. Injustice is an everyday issue that affects the general public. According to the World Justice Project, five billion people globally are affected by some sort of injustice.

The first day. I protested walking with my mask, the one used in the movie called V For Vendetta, and an anonymous custom-made flag walking alone. I started down the road where my brother got killed, then turning right on the pasta plant back road as I reached highway 281, also known as 67th Ave. NE. I eventually ended up on main can't recall the whole walk. I am sure people were thinking. I was out of my mind and/or intoxicated in some way but was sober as a judge.

I have been planning this for a few weeks, building the courage up to carry it out. I don't know what came over me that day, whether it was my fathers' death that influenced it. I had enough to make a stand/or a difference. To this day, as I look back on the event. I must have been wearing them brass balls the counselor had in the center for solutions. For the record, I had no alcohol, illegal or legal drugs in my system. I am proud of myself for the activities I carried out in a sober mind. Whether I made a difference or not. I got exercise, stayed sober, and occupied my mind at the same time.

Carrington is a small town with a population of two thousand, making it more of a challenge. I am sure I would have been more comfortable doing it in bigger cities. In a way, Carrington took a lot away from me, my brother, now my dad. It was time for action. Yes, people were wondering who this guy was? What is he doing? I kept this going for at least a month and, it felt good. As I recall, no law enforcement interfered or made contact with me that I remember, but the state's attorney questioned it. One day I walked past a writer for the local paper I knew from my childhood. She asked what I was doing then started writing a news article about it.

Residents of Carrington who have seen a masked man walking the streets of the city can wonder no more what this person is all about Billy of Carrington is the masked man we have all seen walking about town. He is connected with the occupy movement and is protesting just about everything to do with the government. I am protesting the government, corporate greed, the justice system, and the white house creating bills that take our freedoms away, said Billy. He said the government is trying to pass bills that will censor the internet.

The indicated article is just a taste. I would have to return to Carrington to get the whole paper. You can imagine why I would hesitate to go there. While on the topic. I will share another article involving the passing of Marsy's Law in 2016.

My brother was killed while riding his bicycle in 2008. While I feel that law enforcement did their jobs, I do not feel like others in the legal system did. I cannot do anything to bring my brother back, but if I can do something to help others for the future and ensure that people uphold their duties under the law, I will. I support stronger crime victims' rights for North Dakota, and I encourage you to vote yes on Measure 3 this November. Measure 3 will guarantee crime victims or those acting on their behalf have the right to be notified of court proceedings, the right to be heard throughout the legal process, and to be free from intimidation and harassment. These are rights that my family deserved, and that all crime victims deserve.

My brother's death destroyed my family, and I'm not sure how many people realize how the actions that take one life can harm lives of so many others. Equal rights for crime victims and their families are one way to help lessen additional damage in these awful situations. Please vote yes on Measure 3. (Source: Dickinson Press)

I can only wish victims like me had better rights before but never realized rights never existed tell the measure came to North Dakota. Let us get back on track appreciate your patients.

Anonymous is a decentralized international activist/hacktivist collective/movement that is widely known for its various cyberattacks against several governments, government institutions and government agencies, corporations, and the Church of Scientology. Source: https://en.wikipedia.org/wiki/Anonymous_(group)

Eventually, I grew away from anonymous and was now known as the most wanted masked protester. I gave some masks away and, the owner of the shamrock hung one above the bar whether it's still there or not.

During this time, I also met Big D, a Native American businessman who rented a trailer house from my mom, before meeting him, I was judgmental against Native Americans. I thought they were all the same, but he proved me wrong, showing me that one bad apple shouldn't spoil the rest. He made me an anonymous shirt and would tease me about it a lot. In 2012 he hooked me up with a native chick from the Devils' Lake area wasn't the best relationship. He will be involved, throughout my writing as I call it, for now, because a book would mean writing, is completed, finished, and published. People would see my thinking as a complicated mind.

Big D once said I had a lazy mind. Now with a share of credit to him, it is more proactive in many ways. I believe you have to be a strong-minded person, especially in my shoes, but where there is a will, there is a way. Hopefully, the time I think I wasted will pay off. The woman I hooked up with her name was Rachelle. She had something called lupus, which I can't confirm. She passed away from an accident involving her being on the road and, a car hit her in 2016. Whether she was intoxicated or suicidal, I can't say or remember when I cut contact off with her. She drank a lot more than I could take in. I did break the Bros before hoes code by choosing her over Big D. My and Big Ds relationship was supposed to be tight. I was around twenty-one at the time, young dumb, and full of cum applies here.

Rachelle would be part of my life for at least two years or so. She would live with me starting in Carrington, St. Joseph, Missouri, and Jamestown, where it ended, not because it was a great relationship. I kept hooking back up with her off and on. It is blurry whether I had a place in Carrington or not. I am thinking. We spent time in an empty trailer or at Elmer's rental. She was pregnant difficult to determine me as the father because she was sleeping with other guys, but she ended up having a miscarriage because of her drinking.

Elmer used another friend's truck to drive us to the hospital. The friend's name is Lester, who usually spends a few weeks at a time on Elmer's couch drinking. The motivation behind his drinking is, he lost his daughter while living in Las Vegas and a brother in an accidental fire. Details on both are unclear because too much time passed, and I could not find any news coverage of the fire. Earlier in the story, I did say I would bring him in, and here is an opening. He currently is in his fifties, around Elmer's age, a mystery how their paths crossed. His family owns farmland and rents it out is how he could pay for his bad habits.

Lester's truck got stolen by a guy renting the house at the time. Elmer was staying in their basement, but the brothers abandoned and/or got kicked out. Elmer then took the rent over in return, making him happy. Whether true or not, he claims housing was paying him to live there at one time, maybe an error on their end? The housing authority located in Carrington then relocated to Jamestown, where they re-evaluated his application. Rachelle kept wondering why she had a miscarriage, but it was common sense. She didn't want to admit it was caused by herself? I remember Elmer kicking us out or recommending that we get a hotel room for a few days to have some alone time together. It wasn't enjoyable nor worth the money I spent. It may sound mean or hateful, but that's how I feel now about it.

She remained in Carrington and was staying at a guy's house who she met at the bar. I am thinking she cleaned and/or helped him in some way for housing her. I remember a few times she did drive his pickup to see me. The only reason I was with her was because of the company. I am scared to be alone because part of me is a monster created by injustice. A guy told me he thought I was a homosexual. I am assuming it was because he never saw me with a woman before. She would ask for a shot of alcohol when waking up. I am curious to know what kind of pain she was working on drowning, but later in the story, she would claim I was neglecting her because I was working at Walmart.

Big D was always there for me and impacted my life in many ways. My mom would always suggest that I help him with his projects he had going. If I ever needed help or a place to stay. He has been there for me, but many times, I questioned his motives. I wondered if he is an undercover FED, always making jokes, claiming he is an FBI full-blooded Indian. It seemed like everything went his way in life that he would never fail or accept it. I was only in his life off and on. He was almost like a father figure to me. He would always make me laugh by saying things like I was a broke b***h and asking if I jabbed a girl, which is slang for sex. I'd like to think in a way he saw who I was or what I was like, so he wanted to see me happy.

Guiding my person through life what I needed at the time but hooking me up with that girl was a bad mistake. I am sure neither of us saw the trouble that would soon follow with her, but like I said. I was young. Big D always had good intentions, everything didn't go as planned, and I was still learning in life. He hooked or put me in contact with lots of women while helping him with a convenience store in Belcourt. No, he wasn't my pimp. He would always tease me about giving candy bars away to this one woman, which will be explained further in time. One hook-up took place in Carrington. After the sex, I started to giggle, which may have offended her. It was not my intention to do so, thinking the sex released a chemical in the brain to cause this and/or lack of sleep.

While I met Big D in Carrington, there were other movements taking place around the area. I was getting back in touch with my hometown, where my parents raised me for most of my childhood, which included reconnecting with another girl in my life for a short period. A friend ended up knocking her up then dating her when he knew I was interested in her. I saw this as an act of betrayal. I haven't had contact with either of them since. The last known location for her was Florida, for him still in North Dakota. Her father was a police officer. I either met him there hanging out with his kids or, our paths crossed another way. As a teenager, I was interested in being a police officer and would go on several ride-alongs with him. By now, we both know I ended up in the back seat instead of the front.

I helped him on his campaign to become sheriff, but he lost and later became sheriff for some time. As a young teenager, he got me a pair of fake handcuffs with a badge. I considered him another positive role model in my life, even if it was for a short period. One time he pulled me over whether I was breaking the law or just checking up on me. He then asked me if I was having a sausage feast because of the lack of women in my car, which there were none. I was driving a red ford escort at the time and, the car belonged to my older sister, but she was serving overseas at the time. Later in the years, I would end up rolling it. Luckily, I walked away with no injuries but got cited for reckless driving. It was devasting enough, totaling the car and, now the officer had to write me a ticket too like WOW.

I wasn't drinking during that period. I had my first sip of beer at age fourteen, remembering beer tasted like garbage or, my taste buds weren't familiar with it. Felt the urge to urinate when I didn't have to, indeed a weird feeling. My first time hungover was around age sixteen. The choice of beer was natural ice. I remember it so well because of the puking followed by the dry hives. Around this time, my brother James was also jumped by what I thought were his friends. I did call 911, but for some reason, they never came. I looked for a puzzle piece that fits in some way or another to why he got killed in 2008.

I don't believe I found one, but that's how deep I am willing to dig to find the truth? The police have neglected to perform their duties to protect and serve because of a grudge against our family? James was a suspect in some criminal activity that they couldn't prove back then. Parents were always in denial of it, whether it was to protect my brother or unable to accept the truth either way. Two wrongs don't make it right.

Welcome back was afraid you got lost in the past. Spring of 2012 getting back in touch with New Rockford, which included friends, memories, and places. When I left, it was like leaving all of it behind. I don't know why maybe, I got too lost and/or caught up in Carrington. At this time remember my childhood friend hooking me up with this girl. We only hung out a few times but thinking back on it. I was still hurt, so it wasn't easy for me, and the breakup would have been difficult for me to handle. I did reach out to her, asking what I was like back then. She wondered why I asked. Whether it's a lie or not telling her, I wanted feedback on my person. She claimed not to remember anything. If you remember, earlier I wrote that this writing would remain private until its public release. It's always better safe than sorry. Neither of us pulled hard enough for a relationship to form to this day. She is divorced, with a few kids after, the fact I did start chatting with her again.

One night she was drinking, texting me explicit messages, but it never took off. She was really into me and, then nothing seems to me once a certain amount of time passes. It's harder to reestablish a connection but not impossible. I blocked her for some reason. I was the one that was suffering though she could have tried harder back then if I was worth it to her at the time. I don't think I was worth anything to anyone at the time. I was still lost and/or figuring out what to do with my life. Around this time, I also took a fresh loss in life, losing my dad in March.

I remember being at home on the computer, either looking into anonymous posts or participating in tiny chat rooms while wearing my mask. Whether I was chatting or trolling, I thought I enjoyed it. For readers that aren't familiar with the term *trolling*. In internet slang, a troll is a person who starts flame wars or intentionally upsets people on the internet by posting inflammatory and digressive, extraneous, or off-topic messages online. My friend Bonnie barely hung out with me and/or used me to get revenge on her enemies, coming out of nowhere asking me if I wanted to ride with her to the bar. I, of course, said yes, being an alcoholic and afraid to be alone.

Whether this had to do with my father's death or not, I don't know, but before I left, I made sure my dad had everything, and he was good to go. When I left him alone, I recall he was doing good and showing no signs of struggling with heath that night. History on my father—he was born on April 18th, 1940. He served in the 82nd Airborne, where he might have been involved in the Vietnam War as an Advisor. He never really talked about it much, and/or no records were found online, just hard copies of documents with some information. I remember reading something where he was on an airplane, and he got hit by the loose metal crate, causing him to have a disability, which resulted in him being bedridden. I always remember him swearing at the news a lot and wasn't sure why it didn't change anything.

Back to that night, before leaving, I checked up on my dad, asking if he needed anything else. I was his caretaker. After all, he was my dad but not biological and raised me as his own. I found out when I was maybe twelve. My mom left a case of documents open on the bed, myself being curious, digging through them turned out my last name would have been different if my biological father claimed me. To this day, I never met him and have very little information about him. I won't lie. I never dug deep into it, but who could blame me? He was the one that left me. Should I thank him for the person that I am today? Everything happens for a reason, as they claim. When I was younger, I never believed in that saying, and now I do.

So, my father was all set and I was ready. She picked me up, which didn't take long because we were only three trailer houses apart. We went to the Shamrock. I don't recall any other events taking place this night. I was pretty drunk as I can remember. When I got home, I passed out right away in my room. My mom was working that night so, it was just the two of us. My brother Cookie and little sister were not around or were in Missouri at this time.

As I woke up a few hours later, then checking up on him, and he wasn't responding or breathing. I called 911 as I waited for the ambulance. The dispatcher instructed me to perform cardiopulmonary resuscitation, but I was unsuccessful. The paramedics and an officer arrived, paramedics also performing cardiopulmonary resuscitation or something similar. I remember one of the paramedics saying he must be a smoker, guessing he assumed that from trying to pump air in him? He laughed wasn't sure what way to take or see it now, but at the time, I saw it as disrespectful. The funeral home called the same night too. Like what the f**k was the matter with this guy? I was upset about that. I then contacted my mom. She came home, which is all I can remember about that night because right after, I started drinking heavily. I went to sleep and woke up drinking, never sobered up until I went to jail.

He passed away on a Monday, March 5th, 2012. The next day my mom took off somewhere, thinking she was trying to grief or something. I called 911 repeatedly for some reason. The cops came charged and arrested me for harassment, then a bond hearing. I was released and can't recall any more at this time. There was no autopsy performed, thinking the cause of death ruled as natural causes. After, the fact when looking back on it. What was strange and missing was his underwear, sweatpants, and will. Whether it would be enough to suspect foul play or not but questionable for sure. I wish I could go back in the past mentally... possible, but it would be a challenge. It would surprise me if I remembered every detail that happened that night, nor do I expect myself to, for personal reasons involving my emotions. As I write, edit and finalize the writing, I experience dreams and nightmares from the past.

In May 2012, I took a drive to New Rockford to see friends. I drove around running stop signs and drinking some forty-ounce beers. As I write this, remembering I took other trips while under the influence. I am not proud of it. I remember driving back from Fargo because I got ditched by a friend meeting him in treatment, another time, I was on a back road thinking I must have been tired and drinking. After all, I recollect swerving into and out of the ditch but luckily made it home safe. I was asking for trouble, pushing my luck, and finally got what I deserved. Karma Justice? A person can only get away with something before running out of luck.

I am in the school parking lot across from the school, which was the spot for other friends and me, who would meet up and chat. When the police drove by, I flipped them off with my middle finger. Yeah, not smart, I know. I was asking for trouble. If you remember, my ego was big after peacefully protesting in Carrington. One could consider that as a rise but following behind it was another downfall. I Hung around for a few hours, then decided to take off back to Carrington. IF I thought clearly and had better judgment, I would've left my car there, found a hotel, a ride back, and/or something along those lines, but I choose to drive.

I don't recall feeling the effects of intoxication or anything like it because my body had a high tolerance to alcohol? Joshua could have had a high tolerance as well on the night he took my brother's life. If true, he would've known what exactly he was doing that night. I took the dirt road back and, a police officer soon caught up to me. When I noticed her behind me, I then pulled over, hoping she would pass. Unfortunately, it backfired on me, resulting in her activating the lights and conducting a field sobriety test. I am thinking. I passed but failed the breathalyzer, never recalled taking a blood test, and if my rights were read. Now handcuffed, sitting in the back seat, then transported me to the Ramsey County Jail in Devils Lake, North Dakota. I do believe my brother Cookie picked up my truck at an auto shop in New Rockford. While stuck in jail powerless, he was driving it around with my Ladybird, neglecting my ride resulting in a breakdown.

What are you waiting for plenty of room back here to hear the rest of my story? I wish I could say it ended here, but it never ends with just driving under the influence. No one is ever happy going to jail, am I wrong? There most likely was some pleading and anger involved here with my hands cuffed behind me. A person claimed I am flexible because I slipped my handcuffs from back to the front. The police officer noticing, this called for backup and stopped in Sheyenne. Then an off-duty policeman claimed employment with the city of New Rockford. From what I remember, he never identified himself as a police officer, nor was he dressed like one. Here comes another charge they pulled me out and re-handcuffed me. For some reason or another, I was on my belly in the patrol car. Police then claimed I kicked the male officer with my foot resulting in a simple assault on a police officer charge.

I recall my lawyer mentioning damage that they claimed I caused to the cage, which acts as a divider between police and prisoner transports. We ended up at the jail, once in a holding cell, also known as the drunk tank, I began to act up by throwing my clothes around, causing interference with the cameras, and in return, I ended up only wearing my boxers that night. I don't remember if I bonded out the next day, thinking I was in there for at least sixteen days. When transported by the officer that I allegedly assaulted, I never recognized him, but he claimed he was the one that night. As we are, communicating with each other, he said he would talk to the state's attorney about dropping the simple assault charge. Unfortunately, it never happened.

While I was out on a thousand-dollar-cash bail posted by my mom during those sixteen days, Ladybird forgot about me, which hurt a lot. She did recognize me eventually over some time. She probably thought Kookie was I, for the following reasons. He was driving my pickup, where my scent remained, and him returning in MY pickup. I can't recall if she was with me that night, maybe because my mind is blocking her out since it hurt when I lost her in 2017. Even though she was just a dog, she was a part of my life for about ten years. The thought about losing her or anyone else that I get close to would bring me back to the past, feeling the pain I felt in 2011. When diving into your dark past, I warn you not to stay in the pool filled with darkness for too long. I wish I had better words to describe this.

I remember my lawyer making the argument that I was secured in the back seat, thinking there was no reason to handcuff me again, which resulted in the simple assault charge. Looking back on it, I should have fought harder for a jury trial because I never knew how much a felony would impact my employment and other rights like processing a firearm. I went along with my attorney's advice, not thinking for myself, but

I can't say I didn't deserve it. On a positive note, I made a good Christmas present when released on or before the day of Christmas.

According to court records, I got arrested in Minot on the 9th of September, where a traffic stop took place. I was in a turning lane, but instead of turning, I went straight. The officer claimed I ran a light as the reason for the traffic stop. I was driving with Big D as the passenger because he was tired and with my license suspended. I got arrested and taken to jail. There was either a high or no bond set for my person, and he couldn't stay in town because he needed to be back to work the next day in Dickinson. I spend the night here sober. If I remember correctly, I pleaded guilty because I wanted out of there. Now, if I pleaded not guilty, the courts would have set bail for my release. I got sentenced to serve four days that I never served or was worried about it. There were fines, but I wouldn't have to pay them until later because they had put a hold on my driver's license.

When I would attempt to get my license back, I managed to escape the jail time but not the fines. The court's issued a city-only warrant, but there was a traffic ticket tied into their fines somehow, which eventually went to collections a year later. For my license to be released, fines needed to get paid in full. I won't lie or hate; it was a smart move, whether done intentionally or just a coincidence. How I got back, you ask? At first, I attempted to hitchhike but wasn't having much luck. They make it look simple to do in the films, so I ended up heading to Walmart, where I waited for Big D throughout the whole day to get off and pick me up. For some reason, Walmart always feels like the place to be when stranded.

Again, if I remember right, I was in the Dickinson area with Big D and Rachelle, all of us staying in a camper. I got rehired at the same scrapyard I worked at in 2010. I was learning to operate an escalator picking up piles of iron with a magnet. The operator before me was working as the shop assistant. We switched spots due to him having a stroke, heart attack, or something along those lines. I am sure they thought this was a slower paste job for him, and/or he would be closer to people just in case there was a repeat in history. If not careful, working in a scrap yard can be dangerous, forgetting to mention as they would call a near miss. The operator of an excavator was chopping metal. When he cut a piece of metal, the other half broke off and flew into his Plexiglas shield shattering it. He managed to walk away with no injuries but was in shock, and luckily there were two shields in place.

Eventually, Rachelle got us all detained while we were on our way to pick up some pizza. She was on the phone with 911, which I suspected at the time but didn't say anything. I began to notice all these police cars circling us like sharks in the water. As we arrived at this pizza place, the police moved in, them telling us we were not under arrest but handcuffed and detained us. Police then took us all to their station for further questioning and, the fourth person that was with us got scared and ditched quickly. Big D checked into the jail for a charge later dismissed. The investigators thought he was Rachelle's pimp. I was questioned, cooperated with them, and then released after a few hours but had to walk back to the camper. Police themselves committed a crime that night of theft stealing, a time that I will never get back from them.

Big D's boss came asking about him, caught me by surprise, unprepared to cover up for him, so my response was the truth. Big D then got fired and was forced to leave because the company owned the campground. I somehow ended up back in Carrington. He was still in jail. I was drinking in the bar with his girlfriend for some reason or another. She wondered how to get back at him because she was jealous after discovering a girl was staying with us, so that's when I open my mouth and say you could sleep with me. I know what you're thinking, what a horrible friend, which I agree I was. The guilt I held from the act of betrayal begun to be overwhelming. One night while intoxicated, I told him the truth. We committed the act of betrayal in a storage shed my parent rented because we didn't want anyone knowing about it. In my defense, I never performed well that night because of multiple reasons that played roles in my performance.

The reasons, ranging from being emotionally damaged, having a guilty conscience, being under the influence and the environment, which the betrayal act took place in a storage shed in Carrington. The act of betrayal may have created strong hate towards my person, not only that I betrayed him, but also her trust by coming clean, two wrongs making it right in this case? Big D claimed to be all right with it, but I still hold resentment and/or regret for what I have done that night. In time, I wouldn't be able to drink around them and/or at least while helping him during the powwows. In exchange for this, I would eventually be motivated to cut down on my drinking.

Powwow, a celebration of **American Indian** culture in which people from diverse **indigenous** nations gather for the purpose of dancing, singing, and honoring the traditions of their ancestors. The **term powwow**, which derives from a curing ritual, originated in one of the Algonquian nations of the Northeast Indians. (Source: https://www.britannica.com/)

Spring of 2013, I ended up taking the bus down to St. Joseph, Missouri, not sure what motivated me to move there. At one point in my life, my sister Amanda and brother Kookie stayed there with my older sister at some point in time. Thinking it was my turn to visit for a while, it would be my first time out of North Dakota. While here, I wish I could say I didn't think about Joshua, but he must have filed to get his probation terminated early. My lawyer called and couldn't remember the conversation but did this guy wait until I was out of the state in return taking advantage of the movement? According to my mom, the sheriff served her the papers, but I never been served personally, nor would I have allowed for early termination of his probation. One question I asked earlier does this still sound like an accident?

Once I arrived, it was at night. My older sister picked me up with her red car, happy to see me, this taking place when she was normal or in her right mind. It was nice to be out of North Dakota for once. My sister hated the state but now her currently living there. I stayed with her family, which included her husband and their two kids. They had three kids all together, but I don't recall when James was born. I think he was born after I left. I would babysit a lot until I got a job at Walmart. One thing I noticed about the unfamiliar area. They sold alcohol everywhere, including in the dollar stores, which never help my drinking. To this day, we both have a choice to keep in contact. My door is open for communication, but she lacks to take advantage of it. Without getting too emotional, could it be possible that she experienced a downfall? The thought of myself being absent while physical support is essential in the area. My point here, I don't recall a lot of events with Ladybird, so could the two be related, us switching spots? Is her mind blocking me out?

April was my hire date for Walmart. I remember how I secured the job since they are strict on their criminal background checks. I believe they randomly picked me to undergo the background check or a drug test, luckily ended up taking the drug test. I passed the drug test with flying colors and was hired on as an unload-er but switched to overnight stocking because my brother-in-law was the supervisor. I could have lied, but why did they ask that question in the first place? I would be an unload-er later in time when I traveled back to North Dakota.

When working as an overnight stocker, it wasn't too bad except that their expectations were set too high in my option. Tasks, as they would refer to them. Them expecting employees to complete tasks on time. They never counted the time lost due to the following reasons, disorganized shelves, providing customer service, and the way carts or pallets were stacked, which all consumed extra time. My customer service at a high point here. One time I ran after a lady because she was looking for something, but we couldn't find it at that moment, she gave up. As I continued to look, finding the item, then the chase began. I successfully located her with the item in hand. People may question my work ethic, energy, and overall person, but I choose to go above and beyond. A change people would not welcome because it scares them, in return making them feel uncomfortable.

Everyone forgets about ME comes into play here. My brother-in-law forgot to pick me up from work one morning, so I had to walk back because buses were not running that day. Another example is family forgot my birthday, taking place in Carrington. I brought my mom and sister to Cowboys Pizza for lunch, catching them by surprise, and told them today was my birthday. They were in shock but. I give my mom a pass since she has been through a lot.

After some time passed here, Ladybird and I have united together again, whether that was the motive for the visit, I don't recall. Both were excited to see me. Unfortunately, another person came down this year. The ex-girlfriend Rachelle came back into the picture because I bought her a bus ticket, which was another mistake. One night while I was trying to sleep, she started making out with my roommate. If I forgot to mention it earlier, she also made out with Elmer. When Elmer brought this to my attention, I thought he was lying until he said she spit beer in his mouth, the same thing she had done with me. Later on in Jamestown, she would cheat on me AGAIN. Whether the third time of hard evidence of her cheating on me was the charm or I got fed up with putting myself through this, Jamestown would be the last time we would be together.

My roommate, an ex-coworker of mine, was fired for some reason, maybe because he made out with my ex or he was too slow? While living with my sister, I thought it was a good idea to move in with him. At the time, we were living in a trailer house that he claimed to own. Whether true or not, we eventually got kicked out for a reason leading up to the police showing up one night. I remember talking about Rachelle with my brother-in-law at our work. He made me realize I kept repeating history, causing damage to my person by making the same mistakes with her.

I may have thrown some curveballs in the last paragraphs. I hope you're not stuck there wondering where I was going with it. Missouri is still a scattered puzzle of a mess in my mind. I would save both of us some time and skip it, but try to follow the best you can. While growing up, I always thought bed bugs were a myth until I came here, discovering them hiding in my coworkers' chair, which got thrown out. A tip to the readers. IF you pick any furniture up that has been outside, better kill every bug that may be in there. Bed Bugs are a nightmare to deal with, causing a lack of sleep due to extreme paranoia. When we got kicked from the trailer, we later moved into a house that I alone couldn't afford. Rachelle went back to North Dakota. After she left, only three of us were living in this house.

The two were unable to maintain employment resulting in me moving back in with my sister. While I was gone, other roommates (non-human) moved in with my sister, their place crawling with bed bugs and roaches. I never had experience battling bed bugs, resulting in myself going crazy. I couldn't stand them anymore and requested a transfer, which got approved. A person usually would have to wait six months, but I am thinking it got approved since I was moving. My mom then came down, picking Ladybird and me up. Before going back, I had to make sure not to bring any bed bugs back with me, taking the precaution of washing all of my clothes, which was successful. I drove on the way back, even with my license under suspension or revocation, but we changed seats once close or in North Dakota.

I am now living in Jamestown, at first living with a friend that thought he was married to my mom, so in his mind, I am his stepson. Whether he had a mental illness or not, he was very supportive. Bill is his name, him helping me obtain an apartment. I can't recall if I had my dog or if they allowed pets. I must have had a whole heap of excuses because a coworker I rode with said excuses were similar to assholes. Everybody had one. While living here, I experienced my first fire, even though it took place in a downstairs unit. I woke up to see smoke then panicked, wondering what was going on, thinking this was where my fear of the dark began and/or created.

Since you were thinking it, YES, Rachelle came back in the picture here, but it would be the last time. AGAIN I was sleeping or trying to when she invited a guy in and, giving him a blow job, I confronted her about this she claimed it was a hand job, not like that is any better??? Later her moving in with someone else but would always try coming over. I remember seeing her in the hallway for some reason, whether she was drunk or out of her mind. All this was hard to deal with but somehow managed, or I was piling it up for another 2011.

As I predicted, it's another 2011 all over again. I started to cut myself instead of branding, changing methods for some reason. I then called my sister in St. Joseph, Missouri. I informed her of my intentions, which were to walk into Walmart where I worked, bleeding from the cuts on my arms. At the time, I am thinking it was to show them how much they were hurting me because I had invested a lot of pride in my work. Once I arrived, the police met me at the door, thinking my sister gave them a heads up. I encountered the police multiple times, the day in question. One encounter included me telling them I had a warrant, but it was the city's only warrant in Minot, so it never came up on their computer. I ended up back at my apartment and went out again. Once they realized I kept coming back, they took me to the state hospital, where I talked to a specialist about my brother's death.

After I told her my life story, she decided to keep me overnight, but I had other plans. Once she left, I left, then finding the nearest exit and escaping. As they called the police, I called my mom. The police officers searched for my body, which they never located. One officer got close, being only twenty feet away from me. All this takes place out in a field. My mom located me out in the field, where she picked me up, then went to my apartment, leaving my key without notice and leaving without a trace.

Carrington—I was here for a bit. Big D had a convenience store that he needed help with, so I headed to Belcourt. The store was successful with my support and growing at a fast pace. Big D's girlfriend still held hate against me. One night while drinking vodka, I had an idea to show her and everyone else that I was like them, wanting to earn their respect or approval. As I continued to drink vodka, building up courage, I grabbed a tire iron then headed up to the casino, finding a government-owned truck, where I busted out the taillight. After I went inside the casino and ran into Big D's brother, a security officer, I then bragged about it. After my foolish actions, he called it in over the radio. He would later make comments that I was fearless, having a lot of guts and, he still loved that part where I wanted him to throw me down in the parking lot. Him further saying he is glad that I lived and having a lot of great memories. He does not see me as color, meaning I ain't white? Or he doesn't see white. I can't recall everything that took place this night.

After he called it in over radio, he then takes me out to where I did it, soon cops come arrest me put me in the back seat. Oh no, not another 2012? Middle window was open, I then slipped my handcuffs up front and started crawling through it, as I got into the front and almost out the driver's door, they caught me. I don't recall if I tore up their cage as lawyer claimed in 2012. I was charged or indicted federally for it but dropped in exchange for plea deal resulting in pleading guilty to destruction of government property. They released me to my mother but was on pretrial probation until I was sentenced, sounds made up yes but is real.

I was back in Carrington for maybe a week or two then headed back to Jamestown staying with my father Bill that drove a sweet looking car was yellow Oldsmobile if I remember right. I then ended up gaining employment at Russ Davis Wholesale picking items for lists, operating an electric pallet jack would start with the heavy produce at bottom then light on top, then wrapping the pallet dropping it off at a staging location until it was ready to load in the trucks. Company did pay good every week with good benefits, good job to build mussel while getting paid, loved it a lot but eventually quit it like my other jobs. I do regret quitting this job but drinking was still in my life like I was married in to it.

Eventually I went back to Carrington and was missing in action, my probation officer eventually found me at my mom's trailer. Father Bill told him I was drinking and in possession of a firearm leading to violation of my pretrial probation. Whether true or not it was never confirmed but he would call up mention that they were on their way, that is when I figured out he wasn't coming alone, three federal probation officers show up strapped and ready for a fight. They searched the trailer house very good found nothing, now it was time for the talk, he told me he wanted me to check in a halfway house. I did have a choice ended up picking Fargo, since it had more resources like a addiction treatment center but don't remember it so it must have not impacted me too much.

During winter of 2015, at this time we drove up there in the red Ford pickup, driver's window was broken for some reason and it was a hundred fifty-mile drive. We were prepared though wearing coats, having blankets wrapped around our bodies, plastic covering the window.

On our way up to Fargo, arrived at the halfway house got my stuff unpacked, gave my mom a hug and maybe a kiss on cheek, then said bye. I waited for a while tell they were ready to do the intake for me, while there I was staying sober for a while, drinking coffee mellow yellow, which were replacements for booze at the time.

At the halfway house was first time I was exposed to a card game called spades, which I still love to play but don't plan on going back, so I could play it again. Meant a veteran that had the same name as my daddy Bill played a lot of rummy and other card games with him. Had my own locker everyone wanted to bum cigarettes off me to the point where, I only carried two in my pack at a time to throw em off because I do have a kind heart that others would take advantage of.

This is also when I ran into Marcus what are the ODDS of this happening, played Xbox with him not sure if we talked about my brother. A reminder Marcus was the person with my brother when his life was taken. I do remember other clients fighting over the television to watch sports but Marcus wanted his x box. Also another time, I and other clients my age were laughing our butts off about something, we all ended up getting drug tested that day. Speaking of drugs, clients would smoke synthetic marijuana to bypass drug testing, clients that smoked this would end up strapped to a stretcher.

I heard Marcus tried it and thought he could climb the walls; another person that smoked it thought he was a fairy, due to the fact he entered into another room and threw a lamp at a guy. Maybe he was thinking this was a bag of fairy dust? For some odd reason I never forgot a lot in this period currently on auto pilot typing, if that is a thing? I ended up meeting a lot of people eventually got a job at a place called pizza patrol, I would have to say I would prefer to eat there over Centre and no I did spell it right, which was the name of the halfway house at the time. I'd refuse to get a job for the longest time because I didn't like to follow their unreasonable rules and/or was rebelling a lot. Clients also had to give Centre a certain percentage of their paychecks, whether this was right or not, I will say we were forced to stay there in a way.

One program I hated was called (T4C) Thinking For a Change, yes it was as dumb as it looks and sounds. I myself felt like I was being laughed at for their personal entertainment, they would have you put a finger to your head and say something like, I am thinking I will do better in my life. My probation officer was upset that I made a choice not to participate, I did tell him my reasoning for it. Most people would have done it or anything else to satisfy them but I was the needle in the hay stack. Description Thinking for a Change (T4C) is a cognitive–behavioral curriculum developed by the National Institute of Corrections that concentrates on changing the criminogenic thinking of offenders. (Source crimesoultions.gov)

Eventually I was sentenced to two years supervised probation. From what I heard I had a good probation officer; was this luck again? He was a good person but I just pushed him and certainly paid for it as writing continues. We had to wear wrist bands with names and bar codes on them, scanned us every hour or four they also had random failed computer system checks, that would randomly select clients for drug testing and/or searching, same person would get picked twice in a day. They did not know it at the time but we were being breathalyzed with faulty breathalyzer, which will be discovered as I go on. Those that don't know what a breathalyzer is, it is a machine that detects traces of alcohol. I remember over hearing phone calls, when someone would call asking for a person, the guards or techs whatever you wanna call 'em, their response would be we cannot confirm or deny if that person is here. What there reasoning was behind this? Your guess is just as good as mine, thinking it was an easy way of denying information to the public.

I cannot confirm or deny if you made it to this page. I was able to smuggle alcohol in successfully, nor am I able to confirm or deny it. While serving time here, spades were being played here, there may have been gambling involved. Thinking the coffee was decaffeinated down stairs were the inmates and/or clients, a mix of federal and state, upstairs is where the homeless veterans stayed. One client that was a friend at the time would always tell me I was too emotionally while intoxicated, I don't remember his exact words but I was rising too quick in there but would eventually fall and/or get caught. There policy seemed to be a one strike and you're out depending on the offense. Remembering a few times I may have missed treatment due to being hungover, I was supposed to fail but they passed me just couldn't go on their field trip. There was this one day I went walking to Walmart and this girl picked me up randomly, wish I could remember her name. I had her on a lost contactbook account, she was a good support and most likely would have stayed with her if my escape was successful.

Someone eventually snitched on me for my drinking. At first, they called people from my table that weren't under the influence, assuming they got there information wrong, coming back to apologize, then taking me to the office. When there they breathalyzed me several times, I should have quit cooperating after a few blows, turned out for sometime their main breathalyzer wasn't working. Clients could have been coming back drunk; luckily, I was able to bring the faulty breathalyzer to their attention. Eventually they got the breathalyzer from upstairs blowing numbers and was busted.

They played it off cool, just told me to sleep it off, that morning I woke up as they told me I was on restrictions except for work. As I signed out for work almost out the door, they told me to come back informing me I was on full restriction. I should have kept going but stayed and started thinking of a plan, after lots of thinking and talking with clients and/or friends. The plan was after they scanned us, giving me more time before they would realize I was gone. I was gonna go out get my paycheck and go from there before it could be executed. While in my room chatting, next thing you know two US Marshals show up, everyone in the room had to leave. I ended up having to strip so they could see, I had nothing on my body, then getting dressed and hand cuffed. They then discreetly escorted me out of Centre, claiming they didn't want me to be embarrassed but thinking it was for their benefit not mine. I was loaded up in an unmarked maroon trail blazer and transported to the Cass County Jail.

While there I was able to make contact with my red-headed friend to have him drop my paycheck off, it was successful few days later, I was shackled with belt around my waist handcuffed up front and transported to Stutsman County Jail in Jamestown, North Dakota. Luckily Jamestown was close to Carrington, which is a forty-two-mile drive. Negative side? I was in jail, but a positive side... I was close to my family, probation was getting revoked, wouldn't have to worry about serving my full two years of supervised probation but would have went back in time if it was possible to avoid what was gonna happen next. At a bond hearing they claimed I was a danger to the community reason they used to deny my person bail, even though my crime was breaking out a two-hundred-dollar taillight, was I a danger to other taillights?

As I got there, one of the inmates was playing around with me and/or teasing it would turn out to be. When razors came around for protection, I was able to take a blade out and return razor, but they caught it. Few hours later, they came back and I confessed avoiding a shakedown. After this, I was restricted to not having one, but I do recall a few times the guard forgot or didn't realize it depending on the shift.

The guy whose name will be Erick got close like we were friends or brothers shared my story with him about my brother's death. Remember him getting into a fight over a monopoly game, Erick told another guy playing to shut up for some reason, that's when he went over started beating him, while he was half asleep took the guards a while to figure it out, most likely cause of it happening in a blind spot. When guards did figure it out, they took Erick out to clean him up and keep an eye on him. Erick is currently serving time in Colorado set for release in 2022. I was writing him for a while after I got released but suddenly quit thinking the reason was it was too hard to go back there in my mind.

I did attempt to recently write him but never finished or send it off Soon started making hooch but would get busted for it thinking someone snitch, if you're not familiar with it. Prison-made hooch is a concoction of prunes, oranges or fruit cocktail, sugar, moldy bread, ketchup and water, brewed in a plastic bag. The mixture is allowed to ferment for several days, then filtered through a sock or other cloth to make a crude alcoholic beverage that reportedly tastes as vile as it sounds (source www.google.com.

While I was in jail, my family did visit not sure if it happened or not but told my sister where to walk my dog, which was a spot where I could see her from outdoor recreation, which was on top of the roof of the jail. I soon got the nick name Billy two guns, earned the name working out I am thinking. Eventually, I went to court and was sentenced to three months of incarceration, I remember waiting in the holding cells at court house was not fun at all and/or comfortable. A guard on transport had a nick name inmates called me Bruce Jenner thinking it was how he looked physically, pretty sure he was a male guard though. Every time we got transported, we were shackled by our ankles belt around waist handcuffed up front, holding cells were all metal and concrete it was either standing or laying on your side while you waited. I served two months in county jail, if you're thinking I was gonna finish out my time here, both of us would be wrong.

I grew impatient started to email the jail administrator but was not getting any solid answers. One day they came and called my name, I was excited to be going somewhere maybe a halfway house? Once we all got chained up, they said we were being transported to Sioux Falls then air lifted from there, I was thinking okay for real? Like a field trip maybe even though I didn't have much time left. Our money went in a so-called black box whatever that meant, I don't know but maybe had like five hundred in cash never received it though, until the last three days before my release date which was 06-02-2015.

I do believe we made a few stops to pick up other inmates before heading to Sioux Falls, where we were loaded up on an airplane. If you ever saw the movie con air with the guards in a circle carrying shotguns, yeah it was just like that. This would be my first time on a commercial air plane remembering another inmate saying he saw duck-tape on one of the wings. The only other air plane I flew in was small one and I was in the civil air patrol at the time remember the sick feeling maybe was fourteen at the time can't remember though.

So, we were loading up getting ready to take off I just stared out the window, so I wouldn't get freaked out. I could have just closed the window if there was that option can't recall, either way never thought my first flight would be with con air. Again, made other stops to pick up more passengers on our way to Oklahoma City, percentage of us passengers went to federal holding in the city. The rest of us went to overflow in Grady County Jail in Chickasha, Oklahoma.

One thing I noticed here besides the sliding plexiglass doors and the other people was the food; it was different the meat was a lot darker compared to the north overall, I'd give it four stars would have preferred to finish my time out here over Chicago, where time went very S L O W. I also learned some Spanish, why not take advantage of it?

They called names every day, I was there for a week before they called mine, I will never forget the box they carried all the chains in, we were like cattle in a way. One by one we would step forward strip down naked, get dressed then chained. Once again ground transported by bus to Oklahoma City, then loaded on airplane made a few stops, I and others got off in Rockford Illinois; why not Chicago? I have no idea but we were ninety-two minutes away from Chicago, according to google maps. It would be the longest ninety-two minutes of my life, we were loaded up in three white vans strapped with lights on top, before hitting the road guards made a stop to pick up some snacks, right then and there felt like there was something wrong. As we got going on the road the transport van I was in the tire popped, driver was swerving left to right trying to gain control of it, I was scared for my life thinking it was about to end. Let me remind you we were all handcuffed by our waist and shackled, if we rolled no question of us making it out alive.

I don't understand why it never rolled and/or still question whether I am alive today, maybe in a coma or I am some kind of spirit in the afterlife. That is just how traumatic it was for myself. Luckily, the driver gained control of it, remembering the roads weren't in the best shape and the vans weren't exactly new or in fair shape. For what felt like hours, we all got out where we were gathered in a circle, where they then put a long chain through each of our handcuffed hands to keep us together. Time for guards to secure area each guard on the side of us with a shotgun, another guard walking around playing with is pistol, seemed like a Barney Fife type. For those that don't know the reference I am making, Barney Fife is a character on the Andy Griffin show, where he would only carry one bullet in his pocket because of his excitement to shoot his gun off. What felt like hours in the hot sun, they eventually brought a backup car and/or cars at this point. I started losing my mind making fun of them joking around.

We got loaded up in another van, it only can be described as being in a dog kennel and/or worse without the air conditioning running, we were sweating to the point, where there would be sweat drops forming on roof of the van. Remembering this one guy being forced to wear his coat, as we were going down the road, sometime later another tire on a van pops, we had to sit for some more time. Once we got going again, this is to the point, they started using the sirens, if I remember right not only roads were bad traffic as well. At this point it felt like we were New

York's most wanted criminals, being transported throughout the city like in the movies. We got going again next thing you know a car tire popped whether this was just bad luck or setup who will ever know. Thinking this the time my mind was pushed to think more, if that makes sense, still was acting goofy of course with the mix of stress, heat and stupidity, they never changed the tires themselves, whether they were lazy and/or lacked knowledge is beyond me.

May I remind you all this over a two-hundred-dollar taillight destruction of government property. Yeah, I ain't doing this again lesson learned this was like scared beyond death or something. As we were going up the ramp slow, thank God we were not at high speeds, yet another tire pops on the van I was in, so of course we had to wait for other cars and vans to drop other inmates off before coming back for us. Once we got there had to sign wills in case anything happened to us and donate or send our clothes home, thinking I donated mine cause I didn't want any reminders. I'll say it was a good experience but not another one I'd like to go through again.

A HUMAN, THEN A BUILDING, NOW A RISING STOCK

The food in Chicago wasn't too bad, only reason why I bring it up is cause I am hungry now and was hungry by the time I got there they were giving us sack lunches, which weren't much to give you an idea about the food was so bad that I was losing weight in there. Thinking we had beef stew that night. After a few days here they started to call each person up to let them know where and when they would be going, I was supposed to go to a camp in Oxford Wisconsin.

When they finally called my name, this is what they told me and finally realized. Since you have very little time left, we are gonna have you finish it out here. I was thinking *wow f**k my life*, like really they couldn't realize that back in Jamestown? It didn't get better either: televisions there? You needed radios to hear them. There were four tiers I would call them, top two were gangs one side was the Latin Kings other side I can't remember, bottom two tiers one side Hispanics other side the African Americans and us whites were mixed in all four. Unfortunately, I was bunk mates with a guy I nicknamed Shrek because he was ugly and big.

Those that don't know Shrek is a gigantic, green-skinned, physically intimidating ogre I can't remember his real name or don't want to. Here I was here in this jail I'll call it because that's what it looked like but is considered a prison for federal inmates. Shrek had his own laundry business going; don't fully remember the setup, but there were fans and totes involved. I do believe water came from the showers to fill totes luckily showers were enclosed, provided more protection from Shrek eyeballing my goods.

For those not familiar with jail or prisons guards can smuggle things inside for the right price but for the inmates they would trade commissary items or use them to pay for Shrek's laundry service could range from coffee, ramen soups, toiletries, and synthetic marijuana. I was bored of course inside of a locked building so I decided to help him, in order to make time go by faster if I forgot to mention, time went slow there whether it was based on the environment and/or how intense it gotten from Rockford to Chicago then continuing on the inside. I mainly accepted coffee in exchange for my assistance or my service but always was craving nicotine.

One day Shrek falsely claimed to have tobacco but it was synthetic marijuana rolled up in a sticker, his plan was to get me high off it in return, he could take advantage of me but back fired on him. Whether it was too weak or my mind did not acknowledge the high, it never affected me that I remember. This taking place in the bathroom he said: you know how much I like you, right? Touching my thigh moving closer all I remember right now, only action that I took that I can recall is walking away and going back to my bunk. This would be called a try by other inmates later on next day he acted like nothing happened asking me to help him with the laundry. I told him I just wanted to do my time and leave, then him claiming he was joking around whether I helped him out again can't recall but what I do remember is eventually asking a guard to change beds, he mentioned something like putting me in solitary confinement which I would have been fine with. I would have had my own cell it would have been more of a reward then a punishment for me. Thinking due to this experience, I don't work or do anything in front of new people that I don't know; mainly sticking to myself ain't healthy maybe?

Thinking he said this to scare me from switching beds but it failed, I did get my bed switched ended up on the top right tier felt better where I was. One inmate said I'd be protected never really felt it though but I started employment with him as a watcher and/or look out, making sure no guards were coming while they were giving tattoos. I thought about getting one but never did, they used butter for fire to keep the needle hot, ink may have been from the pens, batteries from radios and other items used to make a prison tattoo gun about all I can remember. I could remember some faces but not many names.

There was this other white guy in there he would always make the joke about getting bisexual, while serving his time here. He soon started giving tattoos to other inmates, there was beef between him and the African Americans, something about him not going through with a tattoo he had promised. One day he came up to the main floor where blood was gushing from his head, this is when we went put under lock-down about a week before I was released. There was talk that there was a metal object involved whether he made it out or not, hard to say.

During my time in the custody of the bureau of prisons, I saw my fair share of violence and am glad to be out, whether it is believable or not. When I was finally discharged or on my way out everyone wanted me to call Shrek out but just walked out in silence and with my head down maybe this whole experience broke me? Got my bus ticket they paid for plus my money that got there the last few days before being released on June 2nd 2015. When I got out, first thing I did was buy a pack of nonmenthol Newports should have got a drink too but main focus was getting away from there, I couldn't believe I was outside and free. There may be more that took place during this period but either mind is blocking them or too painful to process all of the events. Made it to the greyhound and someone asked if I was just released maybe it was the clothes the facility gave me. If you remember I had to send my original clothing to a secondhand store or home. Heading back to Jamestown where I would get picked up and taken to Carrington.

June 2th 2015 I was released from the Metropolitan Correction Center in Chicago, then placing myself back in the community of Carrington, North Dakota. Officially I was out of Chicago, off probation also known as paper. This area of my mind is still messy so bear with me, soon after I got back my former brother-in-law Kyle moved into the area to be around his kids. I remember us living together as roommates. He was working at the chieftain this year.

Our relationship wasn't starting off too bad tell a Mendoza came into the picture, unsure what power she held over guys and/or between her legs but it clamped on to Kyle taking him over. Remembering this one time the hot water heater was out and she would make the kids take cold showers, Mendoza was still married to her husband. He was still in love with her for some reason, maybe just afraid of being alone, starting over again and/or she held the power over him. I remember in one of my drunk black outs, he came over and some sort of fight occurred. I am unsure whether I was involved or not, if I was involved like I would have done anything nor had any energy to defend myself. This should give you an idea of how bad the federal trip affected me. Whether it made me worse or not only you can judge for yourself. I will never know the power Mendoza holds but would it be worth it to find out?

    Earlier when I was in living in Gladstone, Pj's brother randomly attacked me out of nowhere, I never reacted but recalling, PJ saying I was feeling sorry for myself, to be the motive behind it. Whether the reasoning of it and/or many factors could have played a role in it, like being intoxicated, careless, felling guilty, and that I deserved it. I remember Mendoza was staying at a hotel, she invited me in for sexual reasons I am assuming but she was still married, so I never made any advances, again for a number of reasons. Why my person is wired the way he is and/or maybe just a lot I carried at the time, enough self-shrinkage of my mind. In the moment everything was going fine, I remember drinking coffee outside on the deck with Kyle talking about my writing, never really got into it back then, it was just all talk until now. We were living in my parents' old trailer at the time. Remembering myself being at Elmer's feeling sorry for myself drowning in a bottle, he talked me into getting up and snapping out of it. At this time, I think I was only working at the post office, I could have also been working at the restaurant as well.

    I do recall working at the chieftain and leaving unexpectedly, my boss was calling and he even went as far as knocking on my door, which I never answered but do remember joking with my sister Amanda like he was the terminator due to his termination to make contact with me and/or locate me. Recalling myself having never ending anxiety working at the post office, most likely reason for it was because post offices are considered federal. My person would be under the influence to the point, where it would be the new normal for myself and others.

Eventually threw out the writing, I would be able to perform my job sober again. My brother cookie would come over get on his knees and pull his pants down to moon someone, why he did this, I had no idea, he was goofy in a bad way. One night I asked him to leave, him refusing to resulted in myself calling officer Erickson to have him removed, can't recall how many times he had done this, but when it occurred, I took care of it. One day it happened when Mendoza was around, she claimed Cookie was trying to make advances towards her, while Kyle was at work. I didn't see any of her claims she made, if they were even true. Cookie was not doing good in the mental health department in the first place. As his brother felt bad calling the police but also didn't know what else to do, so of course I defended him, when Kyle returned from work.

I can't remember it happening, but I ended up on the floor with Kyle on top of me, he was punching and head-butting me in the face. He would later claim that he just saw red and didn't mean it after the fact. I flipped out cause of all the blood on my head or coming from it so I called 911 officer Erickson responded. Thinking I had a flash back of being back in Chicago, when that guy came to the main floor gushing out blood from his head. Anyways she takes the report I'll never forget this she gave me a choice asking me, if I wanted her to take him to jail. I should have said yes but instead declined, he was still charged but later dropped because I didn't wanna testify, even though they had enough to prosecute him without my help. Whether it was that I didn't wanna relive through it again or I felt that it wasn't fully his fault. The way I saw it is he was a loaded gun and Mendoza pulled the trigger. To this day they are married with another two kids living in Carrington. I have not had contact with any of them for about three years.

After this happened, things were intense for me, even with

the booze in my body thinking he put myself back in Chicago mentally. I should have went to Elmer's or done something differently back then but a person never thinks clearly when they drink. Thinking this happened a few days later on, when as I claimed to be alone at the trailer house, I got shot in my big toe. I didn't call 911; I just called city police directly. Remembering Elmer always saying if you ever needed a ride to hospital just call them, again officer Erickson responds. I don't know why she's the main officer that has dealt with me throughout this story and my life, maybe no one else wanted to deal with me?

Anyways I hopped in her car, telling her I stubbed my toe on a corner, then that a nail caught it, causing the bleeding; could have just soaked it in whiskey or something? When I got to the hospital, told them what happened because they claimed that they would be able to treat it better. Whether this was a trick or not, I wasn't thinking clearly yet again told them I was shot. Hospital then calls the police so, of course, Erickson responds again. She was questioning me. I myself was refusing to cooperate at first, then I just explained to her it was an accident between me and another friend, but she kept pushing trying to get a name. At one point she used a scare tactic that the feds would normally use if they had to, which was a charge of obstruction of justice; was she a fed?

She did make comments like "I knew it was something more" and "looks like it was a 22." I got treated, and later on a sheriff's deputy comes and attempts to question me as well, but I told him the same story. He also worked as a guard in Jamestown while I was serving time there. He ended up taking me home; can't recall if he came inside to look around or not, but a few days later, he would come back with a voluntary search warrant, which I did sign. He was looking around. There was ammunition he found or knew where it was; most likely someone told him. Police never could tie it to me because it was my father's. He then took it, for the reason of myself being a convicted felon, I couldn't be around it. I would have had to get my firearm rights restored. He then asked to take a look in the safe, I replied that I didn't have the combination.

Elmer would later make the joke that I didn't have to shoot myself in order for us to hang out again. For some reason we weren't on speaking terms. The reason may have been that he thought I was gonna kill him because I had a fire poker hidden underneath his couch. I was paranoid reason for it being placed there for my safety, but he thought differently. I do remember doctors telling me I needed to get on blood control and/or alcohol withdraw medication. When I visited them multiple times whether it was the assault or gunshot wound, at the time I was only twenty-five. Isn't that a bit young to be taking blood pressure medication? Thinking I was just in bad shape with everything going on at the time.

Kyle moved out or stayed somewhere else. eventually renting a trailer house, him making a comment of not wanting to be around when people are getting shot. I stayed around for a short period of time but couldn't walk much, of course. Thinking it was best overall to leave due to many factors—avoid being questioned, change of scenery and/or things were just going downhill. Amanda took back control of the post office for a while. I ended up going to the reservation again for what would be a few months. Big D, as always, welcomed my person back with open arms as history continued to show.

Speaking of the devil, I remember us driving down the road sometime in my life, when a deer came out of nowhere, hitting us; the car was totaled. I ended up breaking or spraining my right wrist resulting in myself wearing a cast for about six weeks. It was a struggle living life without the use of my right hand, but another story for another time. Whether you got a sense of humor or not, let's ask ourselves, was this deer suicidal, had a bad day at the office, what caused it to jump in front of a car that day?

Belcourt, North Dakota.

I have been here off-and-on several times helping Big D. I don't know what he saw in me and why he kept helping me out. I considered myself useless and/or a lost cause at the time, but he was not one to give up or throw me away to say. I can't remember what we were doing or had planned this winter and/or early spring. What I do remember is cleaning out his food stand, getting it set up to sell food and making moonshine as he would call it, but it was just apple cider mixed with two hundred poof ever-clear then boiled together, whether this made it stronger I couldn't tell with myself drinking every day. The amount I was taking in couldn't tell whether the booze shot my mind receptors and/or a high tolerance to alcohol. To this day, if I do drink, it is controlled, consuming in small amounts, but if I overdue it, my face numbs a bit.

Since I am on this topic, I have a friend that gets drunk drinking beer everyday gets, like he has no tolerance to it, but he would get sloppy drunk to the point of wetting himself. The story behind his drinking is he accidentally killed his little brother when he was a kid on the farm. Another friend Elmer I am unclear of his motive behind his drinking except that it's fun for him. He moved to North Dakota from California, used to be an egg farmer in Compton, California. Parents ran it but after he lost them, he got into drugs and trouble with the law there. He followed a girl up here was one of many reasons he came to Carrington. An example of being on top one day and hitting rock bottom the next. He still keeps an original business card in a picture frame.

To this day he is doing good, working two jobs saving up money; last time I saw him was only for a hour this year. He maybe wasn't thinking I'd only be there for a short period but another reason for it, I still got warrants there that I refuse to take care of because of the loss of my dog, which you will hear more about as this writing unfolds.

Here we were making moonshine as he called it, never sold it just mainly drank it. In spring of this year 2015, I have a reason to return or escape in Carrington, reasoning I use escape not that he was holding me against my will, it just felt like once I was there I was stuck for the time being but of course I'd keep me too. I am a good worker or would soon to be one. What always drove me crazy about working with and/or for him is he wanted to take on a lot of projects too quickly, whether it overwhelmed me or triggered something in my mind but to this day I prefer to go slow depending on what it is like sex for example can't go right into it. I must slowly get to know the person or be comfortable with them, thinking it has to do a lot with what I have been through in the past.

One thing Big D did to make me uncomfortable was how close he would stand face to face with me while talking to me. Big D s wife would always put me on edge. Thinking it may have been the amount of hate she held against me and/or had a hateful personally towards white people in general. This wasn't the first time nor the last time I'd take off from him but main reason I wanted back in Carrington was cause my little sister wasn't doing good dealing with her boyfriend at this time and she was also involved in drugs.

For some reason we went to Carrington to pick up a machine at the time, we were driving a maroon Tahoe. Why I remember him buying me mellow yellow can't say at this time but when we got there. I helped out for a little bit to move stuff.

While there my thoughts were racing and fighting against each other whether I should stay or take off and how much time I had to make a decision. (at this time auto pilot kicking in) decision was made once I got close to the door, I opened it and ran as far and fast as I could, making it six blocks. Now at my sister's trailer house. They didn't expect me, thinking my knocking was the cops looking for his sister's boyfriend. I can't recall if I knocked or crawled through a window at this time, after I got in. I explained to them what was going on locked all the doors and thinking I was going goofy or something. Not sure how long it took Big D to realize I had escaped whether I was in this mindset because of Fed trip, but he soon came looking for me knocking on the door none of us answered it, of course. He then got mad punched out a window on his Tahoe and then left, going back to Belcourt without me. If I leave a job or a place, usually there is little to no notice given whether this stems from people talking me into staying, feeling guilt about leaving, or other factors; can't really say.

Here I was back in Carrington. I remember taking post office back due to my sister being involved with drugs, making excuses to why she couldn't do it, even though it never took that long to do. The job was three hundred every two weeks for about two hours of work or less, depending on how fast you moved which would equal 12.50 per hour. This is the time I begun to rise to the top having this job then gaining employment at chieftain as night janitor/front desk and at Caseys as a cashier. While I was staying at the trailer with my sister due to the constant traffic flow. I soon started to rent to own my trailer along with Ladybird and another dog that used to be under both sisters' care.

While staying at the trailer with sister, I was involved in a fight I broke up between her and the boyfriend suffering bruised ribs. Remembering they would hurt every time I opened the door to my work place. What hurt the most was my sister was the one that threw me down causing this, they were both raging and whether it was the meth that fueled the fights and/or other factors that played a role. If two people are unhappy, they shouldn't be in a relationship, yes it sucks to be alone but is it gonna be worth all the damage caused both physically and mentally? I remember slamming a coffee cup to the floor is how mad they both made me. It usually takes a lot to push me and their fights have been building up in my head. I just wanted them to end their fights, would start over little things like them dumping each other's plant out. I find myself shaking my head looking back at it.

Why wouldn't she just leave him? A lot of people don't like being alone or unloved. I am sure I played a role in it. I could fully understand the feeling it was not easy for me either but eventually a person can overcome it. My sister at one time used pepper spray on him maybe at one point a taser too that was mine looked like a flashlight. Obtained it somehow from my work at the truck stop her boyfriend is stocky. The rest of his family does not understand how and where he picked up his drinking habit claiming none of the family drinks. He is lucky he is built the way he is, surviving what he's been through.

He has been attacked with a hammer to the head and jumped on the reservation. Hard to say what motivated the attack with hammer but am guessing the person meant to kill him. I wish I could remember more or at-least dig further but from writing this it has gave me headaches, dreams and put me in depression spells. When I am down, could be for a day and/or a week. Just all depends on what it is and how long I allow it to affect myself. Must finish this writing before it finishes me.

What motivated the reservation attack was one native saw him lay a hand on my sister. They beat him half to death from what I saw and heard. He ended up walking down the highway when a driver picked him up and then transported him to the hospital. I can't recall how he made it back to Carrington maybe hitchhiking, though I am sure he wouldn't have had trouble with the shape he was in. Jack was on the Reservation cutting trees down,reasoning for him being there. I can't say he didn't deserve what happened to him or defend his actions, can't even say two wrongs don't make it right here. I later would help him out though something I regret later on doing.

Once I got my own trailer, this cougar chick came into my life, we meant online sharing same interests involving the collective group anonymous. If you remember I was involved with them earlier in my life, going as far as peacefully protesting in my town of Carrington. we had been talking for years about meeting, it was all talk until now action was taken I ended up buying her a bus ticket from Corpus Christi Texas to Jamestown, North Dakota, North Dakota was no bus stop in Carrington, but my dad Bill and I picked her up. We both were excited to finally see each other for her age she was hot and attractive in many ways.

Taking a step back while on the greyhound she missed, a few stops getting frustrated with me, even though nothing happening to her was my fault. I bought her a hotel and did my best to get her here. I remember handing the phone to a regular named Jerry at my workplace. Thinking he came in cause he was bored, but I never minded his conversation. When she called and I was busy at the time working, he took the phone call, then asked me later if she was going through menopause; whether she was or not, your guess is just as good as mine. I was doing my best two-pack; keep her happy buying her cigarettes, which were pall mall reds. She would smoke through a pack or two per day, while going through her addictionbook feeds all day. Thinking her being an addictbook, being in a new area and/or some weed I got for her all may have played roles in her person. I also got the regular stuff people would use like towels for drying off.

If I chose to be cheap would have used a shirt to dry off. I was not being cheap nor did I have a lot of money, due to it being invested in the hotels and her bus ticket plus new trailer house needs like everything. I basically did everything I could in my power to make her feel at home but none of it was ever enough for her. Thinking we were only together for about a week but felt like longer for some reason, maybe how much she was stressing me out? One day she kept texting me demanding that I treat her like a queen in many ways, offered to bring us home a pizza from truck stop but it was not good enough for her. She made threats through texting saying she was gonna kill me or something along those lines. did the physical contact with me drive her crazy? This is not something I play around with, especially in Carrington, so I told her I don't care where you go, but be gone by the time I get home or I'll take further action by having her removed by the police.

After I said that, her tone changed, apologizing and asking if we could sit and talk, but while I was at work, I had time to think about it nor should I have even been thinking about it, should have been focused on my job, but because of her it was hard to do. Remembering making a joke with Michael my co-worker at Casey's about her wanting to give me pillow kisses while I was asleep. Anyways after all I have been through saying that your gonna kill me there is no talking about that, you're gone, one-strike policy.

I used to be one to give a person chance after chance but the chance policy eventually was revamped. She ended up leaving of course, she went over to Jacks for some reason maybe

to stay, while she figured something out. Eventually she got a ride from a city police officer to Jamestown, where both were trash-talking me, of course. I learned of this from the horse's mouth. Whether the cop had me confused with my brother cookie or not hard to say but we have been mixed up before. Reminder my brother was acting goofy out of his mind, likely caused from his drug use. Makes no sense how people mix us up, we are a year apart he has brown hair I got blonde hair alcohol/ drugs more differences. I won't lie I felt a lot better with her gone like a weight lifted. Having relationship both physically and mentally is nice, don't get me wrong, but I was not having the stress that came with it.

I have got an understanding with myself that I must stand my ground no matter the factors involved that play many roles in a thing, person and/or place. Since she left, all I know is the cougar is back in Texas I attempted to find her a few times on locatebook yet never successful but curious to know why she was like that I do know she was smoking weed. Whether my physical contact, weed and/or other drugs played roles in many of my relationships your guess is as good as mine.

Shortly after this I started to build a fence with my co-worker Michael he wasn't only a coworker but a neighbor as well and positive influence in my life. Can't recall what year he moved to Carrington but he rented trailer from my parents he deserves a renter of the year award. He was also a Native

American that never drank any booze nor was he involved with drugs. I needed his help a lot but never remembering him reasoning why is, he was a positive influence in my life. I was still converting from negative to a positive mindset at the time, change is never easy nor does it happen overnight but always possible. Where there is a will, there is a way. Practice what you preach is what I do.

I can't remember if he was compensated for the help but do know my parents knocked off some rent for it, why do I think of that you ask? Most likely it's because he's a really good person deserves a lot of recognition. I feel he is responsible for a big part of me changing my life, making me realize my errors in life. He deserves a lot of credit which will be rewarded in his favor. There were many times I was soaking in my booze drinking every day I would call and/or visit him at the work place.

One thing he said to motivate me to come back to work was: you gotta pay for your habits somehow, right? He was correct, unfortunately. I'll also give credit to my boss at the time; she kept me on the payroll, even though I was hitting rock bottom. I will never forget those that helped me in life, investing their time in ME. They don't know it yet, but they turned a damage human and/or building into a rising stock. There are others that helped me but can't remember them due to my excessive drinking and/or too much time passing.

Remembering is like waking up from a coma, trying to figure out what happened while you were asleep. Me and Michael could have our own reality show; our talks were just that good, the laughing was like an addiction itself. We laughed almost every shift we worked, when it seemed like he was in a bad mood, I would ask him if someone died? Someone left a picture of their grandma at the store, we would tell people someone left there grandma here, them thinking the physical person. A joke in a way some may get it. One night we goofed off so bad if they would have looked at cameras, the manager would have had a talk with us. All that mattered though is we got all our work completed. If there was a reality show I'd have him in it for sure along with a few others maybe.

Okay, let's not drift too far and get back to this fence. At first the plan was to build it around the whole trailer like a heavy guarded trailer house in the ghetto but couldn't due to a fire law or rule. The fence could not cover one of the doors. The trailer house had two doors on the same side; a normal trailer house would have one door on each side, but this one was different, I guess. I was excited about this trailer, though, because it had new hot water heater, furnace, and two bathrooms; it was nice for a trailer house. If things were under better circumstances I would have stayed here but everything happens for a reason. The owner of trailer park Walt was more of an action then a talk kind of a guy, really good guy in general if I needed a place to rent, it be done. He would help me in a heartbeat whether it's because he knows how much I suffered and/or his kind heart, I don't know but do view him as a positive strong leadership figure. So, Walt gives me this paneling for the fence never charging me for it, it was just laying around he claimed, it was a perfect eight-foot-tall sheets.

What was going through my mind, you ask? From the beginning all that stuff I shared with you made my person paranoid. Whether it really happened or not I had a dream that the guy that killed my brother was trying to get into a previous trailer, I was living in let's put that to the side. Look at the facts: he sent me a message claiming my brother committed suicide; there was a false report created that led to my false arrest and imprisonment... later dismissed, whether for lack of evidence or plea deal; and this guy had his probation terminated early and gun rights restored. It's like my brother was never killed, the event never occurred. Yes, he had a power house attorney but still facts remain. This guy did everything in his power to keep me quiet and/or out of town because he felt that I was a threat to him.

Knowledge is power after all. People backed his plate and/or done nothing in my favor is how I felt and still feel. It basically felt like I was alone is reason I had my own trailer two dogs third dog would come in later during the process of building this fence for my protection. I was one person that didn't and/or was not gonna fit in with this town, it feels like a movie called hot fuzz, the plot in there was so many people were accidentally getting killed but a police officer in the movie uncovers the truth. People get normalized to a location never questioning anything I feel this was Carrington and I won't lie I never questioned the so-called accident tell I was giving reason to do so. The guy killing my brother coming into my work place was reason enough for me but not others? So, I get to be the crazy one?

Back to this fence I and my coworker would work on it when there was time, ended up calling the one-eight hundred dig number to get lines marked for digging the holes for the support. I bought most of the lumber for it finding some scraps that were usable for additional support. A neighbor had some tree stumps which were used as well. I can't recall how long this project took but eventually was completed. Around this time a roundabout was under construction in Carrington. I always talked about getting a pit-bull for more security, one day my manager called me away from the tills, in order to talk with a construction worker that was working on the road.

Not having any time to decide on the matter, he had an adult pit-bull right there in the back of store that he gave to me but until I could transport him back to my trailer after my shift, he had to stay in a caged area. My plan was to have this dog not bond with anyone learning from my past, recalling the time when a guy stole my x box in Gladstone, this was a win for me. Many more ahead as well before hitting another rock bottom in 2017 (writers note writing this is like reliving it again gives me feelings of enjoyment.)

This dog had a name that I can't remember right now, but I kept him in enclosed porch area that the fence didn't and couldn't cover because of a fire law. Reason for this is if anyone came in, they could meet him first, whether he would attack or not is another question our relationship was fresh, that's not the only thing he got fresh with. My other dog that I would call Limburger she wasn't fixed and in heat, she tried fighting him off for sometime but eventually gave it up. I wasn't knowledgeable in the dog area, but one day I opened the door to check up on them and they were stuck together. Myself panicking finding the veterinarians phone number, then called her where she explained to me what had taken place and why they were locked together.

Now she was pregnant and always looking guilty for some reason. She has always had that look throughout multiple ownership's for some reason or another. People say dogs feed of your energy whether it holds water or not I can believe it somewhat, she was not a bad dog though picked up some bad habits though. I ended up house breaking her and Ladybird as well it was not too hard to do, just can't be lazy at it. One way I would trick Ladybird was giving her a piece of her own dog food, her thinking it was a real treat. I was happy to have all of them except the pit bull he was a stubborn dog to train. You can't teach old dogs new tricks would apply here.

Limburger probably was hoping or wishing he was gone at the time; if she was, her wish would soon be granted. I was drinking over at Elmer's one day staying overnight, then walking back home and opening my door, the pit bull then escaped. I didn't really care because I was a bit hungover. Someone later made me feel guilty about it so I called the police to locate him, the officer claimed to have a good home for him, so of course I didn't put up much of a fight due to the fact it was not easy to train him and our relationship was still fresh. So this was considered another win for me. Limburger was pregnant and police officer knew of a good home for the pit bull.

Those that ain't familiar with pit-bulls they are good dogs, if trained right while they are pups. Pit bulls like to chew everything up in their sight, I had a bunch of newspapers I was saving up because they were just going to waste. My idea was to make paper logs and sell them, I bought the machine or device but never acted on it. Instead, they piled up in the entryway. The trailer park owner was curious to why, which I could understand his curiosity about it now.

This was not the first time the police took something from me, I had this car parked in my driveway, city made an ordinance using it to their advantage. One day while I was working at my job, I had removed all of my tires from the car putting it on bricks, since they threaten to tow because it had no tags on the plates. I attempted to reason with them but at the end, they picked it up with a pay loader, before they did this, I loaded it up with junk. I figured the car would put up a fight with them since I wasn't getting anywhere with them. Reason I never had the car tagged was that there were problems with it. Once it warmed up transmission would go out. I can understand them towing it if it was parked on the street but it was parked in a privately owned driveway nor did it look like junk. If I had more time to look for loop holes, I would have but was busy working multiple jobs at the time.

At this time, I had an interest in a girl she would always ride her bike to my work place to buy those four pack wine bottles, fireball shots and a pack of Marlboro smooths, if I remember correctly. She would also visit with another co-worker of mine her name Rita, she also played a role in my life. What attracted me to this girl you ask, we had a lot in common. She lost her dad, resulting in us sharing a loss together, never did drugs, drank as well; we both didn't have a license and/or kids at the time. Perfect match, right? Rita ended up hooking us up, I can't remember if I was too shy to confront her, had low self-esteem and/or confidence. Whatever the deal was, maybe I was working on dropping my balls again at this point? First time we hung out, both of us engaged in physical activities like we were met for each-other but would turn out to be like adding gasoline to a fire relationship.

The way it started was that she wanted to keep me a secret but am sure everyone, already knew about us seeing each-other. She would park her car somewhere else and walk to my place, like what makes her reputation better than mine? At this point I was catching speed with my work I remember myself telling my boss that I was working one-hundred fifty percent average among others that were at sixty percent at the time, the way I saw it, I was going above and beyond, operating three tills at the same time, hustling to feel the outside window cleaner and any other problems that came up. I give credit to my federal trip experience in a way they made me think more, my mind got more creative in unbelievable ways. It's a natural experience, for example others can take illegal or legal drugs in order for their minds to be more active. It caused a near death experience for my mind to be pushed more if that makes sense? If I had things to do, I would take care of them right away, so I wouldn't have to worry about them anymore.

One day I was heading out to clean the post office sober. My girlfriend wanted me to stay so we could cuddle, probably her fear of being alone or something. I explained to her it would be real quick, but she wasn't gonna let me leave using her sex as a tool in order to keep me there. Without including too many details, fifteen minutes later, I was back on track, so it basically backfired on her. She would always use her sex to stop and/or distract me as an advantage for her but a weakness for me battles were endless in that area. She would always complain I was too fast, yes it be nice to have a balance. I won't lie it was the start of my downfall or part of it. She seemed to love my animals more than me our relationship was based on drinking. I saw it, but she denied it.

She soon got her license back she would drive drunk though. One night I'd have to leave a shift early to take her home (my place) or her to take me home, since she was driving. She always claimed we never had a serious relationship but was mainly staying at my place, so what does that tell you? This is when I should have broken it off but I was too consumed in it bathing in the booze sex and fun. Thinking back on it she did leave for a short period of time and it was another 2011 all over again. Reasoning for this was love I had for those I lost. I am thinking when she left it was triggered and/or opened, what I call the dark box or place.

My emotions were running wild and untamed thinking I took a few weeks off drinking and acting like a fool, I started burning myself again. I remember crying to a former boss of mine telling her I felt like a loser having nothing because I didn't have a car or my license at the time. This was only a minor setback to my rise but emotions were intense is what Ben would later tell me. Those that don't remember he was my treatment counselor and/or shrink back in 2008–2009. I'd call my coworker almost every night, he eventually talked me into returning. It's not something I like feeling, but whether it was the sex and/or having someone there, then gone the next day activated or opened that dark box.

There are many times I should have been admitted or taken to state hospital but maybe no one cared? But I got through it luckily, she did eventually come back into the picture after I started seeing someone else. I was weak back then couldn't say no or had any self-control. Self-control is a major key in changing yourself but there are different strokes for different folks may apply here. She still loved my animals more than me of course, she was always talking about being a midwife or something, when the puppies were born which took place in December or January.

The day they were being born, I was freaking out didn't know what to do so I called my boss she rushed over and assisted me. At this time, I was talking and hanging out with her daughter I may also been working at the chieftain again. I'd call and confirm but this writing will remain secret and/or sealed until released to the public. Her daughter or the girl next door. She always wanted pain pills for some kind of pain she was having, whether it was mentally or physical. Thinking this is one of many reasons mountain girl came back in the picture was because I was seeing the girl next door at this time. First time sleeping with her was awkward due to the fact I was sober and/or I didn't want to hurt her because of the pain she was complaining about. I had no access to pain pills to help with her pain.

Most my adult life from age seventeen to this point, my

body mainly operated on booze in return being sober was weird and/or new to me. It could be best described as being in prison for a very long time. Once sober and/or being released from prison, it takes time to adapt to the new world, while others may look at you different. Whether true or not you must continue to move forward in your life, making improvements for your person. It will not be easy nor is anything impossible. Depending on your addiction let's use food as an example. My favorite food is tater tot casserole in order to avoid over eating it. I put it in the fridge as soon as possible or you can put it in the oven tell it cools down. No matter our addiction and/or addictions, we all can overcome them. As Ben would say, "I am still in recovery, you could be too; takes a lot of hard work and/or motivation."

Did you get stuck in group? Some feedback I got is I would be a good addiction counselor. Would you guys agree?

Since you're back here, let's continue with our story. When I was with mountain I would shake when sleeping together with her, remembering her telling me to slow down, then asking why I was shaking told her probably because of the booze thinking after that. She told me to go drink a beer after I did it would stop. For some reason she would always ask if I was happy. It bothers me not remembering the reasoning. Later I would consult with my council at the time, which included my graveyard coworkers Michael and Rita. Rita helped me confirm and/or realize that it was the body used to operating on alcohol, resulting in the shakes during performing sober physical activities.

I remember a person having the same problem. What I would suggest is taking time off at-least two weeks, then cutting down slowly. Then you must be around people sober or have a beer or a few, just to get the body slowly but surely adjusted to a sober stage. For example, you got a dog that ain't used to a new person, it's gonna take that dog sometime to adjust to them, right? That dog is like your sober body in a way if that makes sense? Or you can just take pills and detox in a hospital. As I mentioned earlier Mountain left then came back in my life.

I am sure you are curious about the nick name of my ex-girlfriend reason I refer to her as that is because I wrote a short story about us that was never finished. I don't know what motivated me to write this maybe it was cause she opened a bottle of my top brand whiskey, which made me angry sounds silly I know, but I had my top brands and the usually whiskey I would drink. She knew this, maybe she was looking for a rise out of me, well she got a rise all right, whether or not it was the one she was looking for, I can't recall or if she even knew about the story.

Anyways the story is about me living in a whiskey cave on a mountain and she would attempt to drink or steal my whiskey. At some point in the story, she jumps off the mountain because she had to make it to work, at the time she valued her job making a big deal out of being a successful department manager. She wasn't all bad nor was I she would buy me clothes, which was sweet of her. Liquor and/or other substances can change people like all things it has its cons and pros. Drinking gave me courage in a way helped me socialize better but affected my judgment, behavior and overall person.

Normally I am a very quiet shy person. Brother-in-law once said booze brings out the truth or something of that sort. I have attempted to contact her a few times but no response she was part of my downfall and/or influenced it. I ain't denying responsibility for my actions nor am I saying I acted alone. When she would stay overnight for some reason out of nowhere she would slap me hard, while I was asleep, which I can't stop laughing at it because she did the same thing to a former friend now associate of mine while I was in jail.

This is how he told it: I went to my backroom to sleep and she came back there slapped me so hard I saw stars. Myself in jail will be further explained as writing continues. Elmer also told me Rachelle spit beer in his mouth, while kissing him is how I knew she was cheating on me and that he was telling the truth about her. If you forgot she was another ex-girlfriend of mine.

*At this point in my writing it puts us in December 2016. When a snowstorm and/or blizzard took place triggering a shut down in our town of Carrington for a few days, which is bad if you're living in North Dakota. If I never mentioned it my boss was living next door to me in a double wide trailer house. Where Bonnie used to live but then moving out for some reason and into a house strait across from Elmer's rental. My boss attempted to drive her car to work but the snow was too deep and/or wet. I remember getting a good workout grabbing a few shovels to dig her out.

Around this time, me and Michael were coming into work in order to cover shifts because of other employees calling in. I and Michael's regular shifts were working graveyards. At one time I was on the 8–4, day shift, when I first gained employment this year. Thinking the reason I applied is he kept pressuring me whether he was joking or not I applied. Michael usually drove his car but also had a pickup and that's what we needed in order to make it into the job that day. I remember it was hard to see with the blowing snow but we made it there.

I remember this one guy making a joke about the snow plows like them only operating during the day time maybe he referred to them as being solar powered plows? Snow storm did strand the truckers in place for a day or two whether or not the readers would be interested in knowing about the North Dakota winters. Every three to four years a bad winter storm would hit. Thinking about this takes me back to my childhood in New Rockford the snowstorm was so bad, that the wind would blow our back door open resulting in snow accumulating in our laundry room, for some reason we attempted to leave by car but assuming the snow was too deep so we all ended up snuggled in the master bedroom. One thing I always hated about this state besides how they treated and handled the death of my brother was the wind. It was windy almost every day so it should have been clean right, just in case it wasn't we had street sweepers.

February 2017 while I was working my shift at Casey's heard about a trailer on fire from one of our regulars. At first, I was thinking it was my trailer house, worried then calling the police but luckily it wasn't my trailer nor was it close to it. If I remember correctly when finding out about the trailer that was involved, which was rented and/or owned by the son of a sheriff that resigned in 2014 without notice. I never did mention this notice until now nor do I know why multiple people resigned around that time.

CARRINGTON, N.D. – Foster County officials said Thursday that steps are being taken to replace an unusually high amount of personnel who resigned en masse earlier this month.

Foster County State's Attorney Paul Murphy and Foster County Commission Chairman Bill Bauer spoke at a news conference Thursday in the county seat of Carrington in this central North Dakota County. The two also said delayed tax bills should be in the mail next week.

Earlier this month five county officials—Auditor Teresa Rivosi, County Sheriff Michael Tufte, Sheriff's Deputy Danielle Rosewaren, County Clerk of District Court Tamara Becker and Deputy Clerk of District Court Jenna Weisenberger submitted letters of resignation. Tufte's resignation was effective Nov. 30, Rivosi's was effective Dec. 2, and the remaining three officials will be done Dec. 31.

Murphy said he thought the resignations were an unfortunate situation. "We have some holes in our lineup, but we still have to put a team on the field," Murphy said.

Bauer said he didn't know the reasons or the source of conflicts for all of the resignations. The state's attorney said the commission will review the county's general policies and procedures to ensure a quality work environment for county workers. He said he would like to see staff meetings on a regular basis where a commission member attends and listens to what the county workers have to say.

Bauer also explained how the commission will hire a replacement for the sheriff. The position has been advertised in newspapers in Foster County and posted with other law enforcement agencies around the state. After the new sheriff is hired, he or she will hire a qualified applicant to replace Rosewaren, Bauer said. Bauer said the new sheriff will fill serve for two years then have to run for the office in 2016.

Off-duty Carrington Police Department officers have volunteered to help Deputy Howard Head during the first two weeks in January when Head will be the only Foster County Sheriff's Office law enforcement officer on duty, according to Bauer.

As for delayed tax bills, Bauer said Foster County Commissioner James Carr contacted the Office of State Tax Commissioner and had officials there talk with Foster County Treasurer Norene Barton and Deputy County Auditor Heather Martin so they could complete the process for certifying the mill levy information. Barton said Thursday she spoke with an official from tax commissioner's office, and the tax notices will be done and mailed by Thursday or Friday of next week to county property owners.

(Source: https://www.grandforksherald.com)

According to the source this was written on December 11, 2014. I have a lot of questions here, so bear with me. High amount of county employees resigning, wish I had the answers unusually yes. Where do delayed tax bills fit in with this article? Why was it important for them to get that out? How does it relate to county employees resigning? Putting a team on the field? Should be a team of federal investigators if you ask me, something is very wrong here. So off duty police officers are gonna volunteer to help one deputy, like are they gonna go on a two-week vacation is that how it will work? Who will replace those police officers? Maybe volunteer citizens? So, they start and finish article with delaying tax bills. Why are these tax delay bills in a article involving high amount of county employees resigning? Maybe I am missing something did the tax delay bills have something to do with county employees resigning?

CARRINGTON – Foster County State's Attorney Paul Murphy resigned his position Wednesday, and the Foster County Commission will hold a special meeting Monday to go over the procedure to appoint a replacement for Murphy. Foster County Auditor Casey Cables said Thursday afternoon that the County Commission will meet at 9 a.m. Monday. Cables said Kim Radermacher, a former assistant state's attorney for Foster County, has agreed to help the county while the County Commission figures out a way to fill the state's attorney position.

Cables said county employees have also been asked by the commission to consult with the North Dakota Association of Counties on any "legalities." Cables said Thursday that she was walking in the county courthouse when Murphy walked up to her.

"I asked him if he was going to a special meeting the commission was holding last (Wednesday) night," she said. "He said, 'no,' and handed me a letter." The letter was his resignation letter. Cables said Murphy offered no other reason as to why he was resigning. The special County Commission meeting was held to discuss if the state's attorney's physical office should be moved into the county courthouse. Cables said the commission approved moving the office back into the courthouse building. Murphy was operating his state's attorney office out of an office space in his home.

A HUMAN, THEN A BUILDING, NOW A RISING STOCK

Murphy sent out a press release Thursday announcing his resignation. In the letter Murphy, who has held the office since he was elected in 2002, said his resignation "is the product of contemplation of whether or not I should (to) fight a vocal minority, a group that has the power to make life extremely difficult for me."

Murphy said Thursday evening he attended the County Commission meeting Tuesday morning before heading to the courtroom. He said he was only at the meeting for about ten minutes when Commission Chairman Josh Dreher allegedly told Murphy he is rarely at County Commission meetings and that he was going to ask the governor's office to have him removed.

Attempts to contact Dreher Thursday afternoon were not successful. Murphy said he believes that Dreher and newly appointed commissioner Roger Gussiaas don't like him because of past dealings with Gussiaas family members.

He said dealing with the animosity from the County Commission helped him make up his mind to resign. Murphy said he has maintained a small private practice while working as the Foster County state's attorney and will expand that work now that he has resigned. Murphy said he enjoyed his time as Foster County state's attorney and had helped people through his work.

Murphy's resignation is the latest in a series of resignations and firings stretching over a year and a half for Foster County. Between November 2014 and June 2015, nine county officials, including former county Auditor Teresa Rivosi, resigned their positions for various reasons. Cables confirmed that Dreher, Gussiaas and Vice Chairman Pat Copenhaver were all appointed to the County Commission over the last year.

Cables said all three commission seats are up for election this year, and the men currently holding those seats will have to decide if they want to run for those positions. Cables said Dreher's seat was the only one scheduled to be up for election in 2016. If he decides to run again for the seat he was appointed to and wins, that seat will be up for election again in 2020. (Source: https://www.grandforksherald.com)

Multiple paragraphs that caught my attention was a former assistant state's attorney for this county. Did Foster County ever have a spot for an assistant? Was the county bigger at that time? According to google (Carrington reached its highest population of 2,084 in 2012). I will be honest I am lost here maybe the crime rate was really high at one time? As I mentioned through the story, more questions than answers. The office of state's attorney was moved three times strange why it wasn't kept in the courthouse but okay. According to an article, Paul claims people have the power to make his life extremely difficult. I don't know who to believe or how far this city as gone downhill with no notice.

This to me is unbelievable like how did this town fly under a radar for so long? Did the people just not care anymore, maybe there just getting real sloppy now? There is a lot more blogs out there, all this is from news articles. Imagine how bad it really is behind CLOSED doors.

Wow, sorry for that detour. I never planned that to happen, funny that I say that, because nothing that I ever had planned works out and/or goes as planned that I can recall. I never saw the articles and/or noticed questionable comments made in them, like this town is handing me itself on a plate. What I mean is I am writing about it, like there needs to be an investigation launched or something, right? Or will this continue? I am curious as I am sure you would be too or maybe wouldn't wanna touch it with a ten-foot pole?

It is scary, I won't lie; maybe this is the reason my brother got killed; that's what Carrington residents have been leading me to believe so far. Joshua, the guy that took my brother's life caused me to investigate. Are these people gonna blame him? Who are these people that pull the strings? There is a saying about not focusing on one thing, place and/or person. Here I am writing about my life, discovering new and/or forgotten information, like WOW this is great information whether true or not. I am entertained by it. Starting to understand why this true story about my life is secretive?

For real, let's get back on track now. So, this trailer that caught on fire, to my knowledge, a space heater caused it. According to news reports I have read, it started in one of the children's bedroom and/or bedrooms. This is suspicious to me whether it was intentionally set or not. I was questioning it because there were three children who lost their lives in it, the father I am guessing was working at the time. I cannot confirm it though but it would make sense since he went in attempting to save his children, then ending up in a burn unit. The cause of death for the children is unknown at this time, but your welcome to read multiple news articles to find out. I myself attempted to skim through articles but could not get a clear explanation and/or answer. I don't know these people well, except for one that I used to work with at the chieftain. He was a server and their roommate at the time. I will remind you too that my brother's death was claimed as ACCIDENTALLY. Shortly after this tragic event. I obtained my driver's license, resulting in myself continuing to rise.

March of 2017 was when I got my license back. I ended up taking the written and road test because it was inactive for a certain period of time. Last time I drove legally that I know off was in 2012. An associate of mine allowed me use of his truck to take the test. I didn't really know this guy that well, but he was a coworker at the deli at one time. I remember him asking me if I was still trying to put Marcus in jail, which was the guy that was with my brother riding bikes together at the time of his death. I was curious if he knew something maybe Marcus was guilty of something and/or if they were in communication with each other. Around this period is when I discovered an investigator's report surrounding this so-called accident. I am thinking it was found in my parents' old trailer won't say who brought it to my attention. The trailer house was towed away due to a fire someone started inside of it, yes towed away sounds silly but it was questionable. This happening while I was out of state and/or area. Another story for another time.

I felt finding this report was another break in the case but made me more of a threat? Luckily, I was drinking a lot at the time, my drinking may have saved me in a way. So, in this report it sounded similar to the one that was made against me. A report falsely claiming I was stocking a person and/or persons resulting in my myself getting falsely arrested, imprisonment and/or accused for violating the restraining order. In the report it was so well written like the person knew everything that was going on, was this planned out?

Thinking of this raises questions about my brother's death. In the report involving my brother death, a person claims he saw the truck coming, further describes all the turns the driver took. This guy saw it coming or knew what to say.

Premeditated murder maybe?
There was a lot of thoughts going on in my mind at this time, reason to why earlier in the writing I stated that I attempted to get the same report to confirm it was authentic. The lawyer involved with the wrongful death suit and/or with my family claimed that records were destroyed. When I asked for the crime scene pictures, he told me I needed my mother's permission, which was granted but still nothing. I naturally started asking questions again but should have remained silent. This is where I started suspecting Marcus of hiding something from me. Earlier in my life I never questioned or looked at him as a suspect until now. There are other factors that apply here whether they support my suspicions or not. One he didn't pursue in a wrongful death lawsuit against the guy. Two he avoided talking to me about the accident. Three his ex-wife was fakebook friends with Joshua Alan Sherman, the man that took my brother's life away from us forever. Them being fakebook friends establishes some sort of connection in

knowing each other, I feel she is hiding something but what? I don't know, but everyone is staying quiet about it.

Marcus's court attendance is highly questionable whether he was getting off easy for multiple reasons including he knew of someone in power, a criminal informant and/or was just an upstanding citizen. I don't think it's because he was a upstanding citizen. His criminal record according to the public access site is way longer than mine. The last case he was involved with resulted in the death of his own son. According to the news articles them claiming Marcus admitted in open court that himself providing meth to the mother. Oh no Marcus involved with another death? Marcus was never charged for contributing to the death of his son. He must be in good standing with the courts since he is so comfortable about them knowing is location which is listed as Vancouver, Washington. Now let's say he was getting lucky why would he keep his address updated with the courts? Five felonies listed and a long list of misdemeanors. How is this gonna make our courts look in North Dakota?

I don't know about you, but something is very wrong here. Whether this is faith why I gained this knowledge or someone pointing me in the right direction. Before this I would have never thought to even look at him as a person of interest and/or would anyone else see this coming? If I can see this, which I remind you, it is record of public information. Why couldn't anyone else see and/or notice this pattern?

Once again, more questions than answers. Funny thing is I was writing this girl when she was in prison and had plans of hooking up with her after her release. She actually was the one I lost my virginity to. But due to a change of events, I was not in the area, and she was so quick to hook up with Marcus. Whether this suspected corruption is in Carrington or widespread throughout the state? Who knows? What I do know is there should be an investigation done starting in Carrington. Did my brother see or hear something he wasn't supposed to? Slept with a girlfriend? Motive would be hard to establish at this time due to the lack of information and witnesses or their fear of coming forward.

UPDATE: The Carrington woman charged in the death of her four-month-old son last July, plead guilty to two felony counts early this morning. Twenty-five-year-old Justice Lange was originally charged with manslaughter and one felony count of child neglect, but a plea agreement changed the first count to negligent homicide— keeping the second charge the same. A Stutsman County judge sentenced Lange to twelve years in prison with two years of supervised probation. Due to her long criminal history, the state asked she be deemed a 'habitual offender,' making the maximum sentence double in both charges. Lange and her four-month-old baby, Tyr, went missing for six days last June into July. Her baby was ultimately found in a slough in rural Stutsman County, with an autopsy showing he died of starvation.

After hearing from both the state and defense, Lange addressed the court—taking 'full responsibility' for using meth and the death of her son, but also blamed her ex-fiancé for giving her the drugs in the first place.

"There's no words that I can put into it, because it's affected my life. And nothing that you guys can give me is ever going to amount to what I do to myself every day," Lange said.

However, those comments did not sit well with Judge Cherie Clark. Clark told Lange she didn't feel like Lange showed enough remorse or guilt for the crime against baby Tyr, adding that Lange should have expected harm to come to her son the moment she took meth.

"This child completely trusted you for its life, for its health, for its food, for its water," Clark said. Those words visibly upset Lange as she clenched her fists and closed her eyes as the judge continued to talk. Judge

Clark became emotional herself and called for the courtroom to sit in a minute of silence "to think about the last minute of (Lange's) child's life while it was starving to death, after being exposed and having no water or clothing for six days."

"Your conduct killed your child. I just keep thinking about the last hour, minute, second of your child's life and it causes me to lose sleep," Clark continued. Lange's ex-fiancé, Jason Wilde, was telephoned into the hearing. He was very emotional, saying he'll never understand why she did this and he'll always miss his son. He admitted to getting meth for Lange, but he says it was because Lange asked him to. Judge Clark handed down a slightly longer sentence than what the state and Lange had come to in their plea agreement. And because of that decision, Lange now has forty-eight hours to decide if she will take the judge's sentence or if she will withdraw her guilty plea. Source www.valleynewslive.com

---

This taking place in or around July 4th 2018, is what caught my attention because I lost my brother July 6th 2008 around midnight. So, I am thinking Marcus was maybe thinking of the anniversary of my brother's death needed meth to forget about it? What other reason could it be that this occurred on and/or around that date. If you notice news mainly was focusing and/or taking an interest in the mother at the time, but for Marcus to put himself in a spotlight like that is a foolish and/or sloppy mistake on his part.

I cannot remember the exact date but it happened during these years. I did confront him about the investigators report. After I did, he wanted to see for himself going to talk with the state's attorney. Whether he found anything out or went there to make himself look good, I don't know. What I do know is what I read, heard and saw. Lawyer's son was part of the conversion at the time so whether his death was related it continues to puzzle me but questionable yes. Since I saw that message from the guy that killed my brother stating my brother committed suicide by riding his bike in front of his pickup.

From then to now, every single suicide that took place and/or that still occurs there in Carrington will be suspect to me whether there's foul play in question or just the fact the message makes my mind like that. You as the readers decide it's not what I know but what I can prove. I strongly find there is enough information for an investigation to be conducted. I don't intend to get off topic but while it's fresh in my mind, this alone I can make a book off. If a suicide happens there would be little to no news coverage on it due to respect for the family. Was Joshua hoping to get my brother's death ruled as a suicide?

Back to my timeline after another short detour I finally had my license back. How long I'll end up keeping it you will find out. I was excited about it felt better about myself. If you remembered my short down fall after mountain left? I was back on track rising to the top as I like to call it. Now I needed a car this one regular was always talking about selling his ninety-nine Crown Victoria police interceptor. Now what caught my attention with this car was I wanted to be a police officer when growing up and/or felt this was another home for me. Using as a joke since I was in and out of a police car multiple times in my life, being in the backseat instead of the front. He sold it to me. I felt comfortable with the purchase because police are known to take care of them, like having regular maintenance performed on them. Another reason is I felt this guy took good care of it as well either way I was excited regardless. I remember this coworker would tease me, saying how long I would be able to keep my license before losing it again.

After owning this car, renting to buy my own trailer house, paying my own bills, having a fence around it and/or having three dogs, two good jobs and one girlfriend. I was set and on top of everything how I saw it. I would learn after the fact that I rose too quickly resulting in a hard downfall and/or rock-bottom. On or around April 10th 2017, I received a charge of driving under the influence, while only having my license over a month. Thinking I was showing off being fearless or my ego was too big because of how high I have rose at that point. Yes, I was still drinking everyday but it wasn't as bad as I thought. I remember going to New Rockford to hang out with my little sister and her friend Kenny. Kenny was in his late forty's also Bonnie's brother can't recall how their paths crossed. I was drinking there, then decided to head back to Carrington for some reason. I am thinking it might have been to hang out with the girlfriend or as I refer to her as mountain. My sister makes a claim that she was willing to drive back that day, whether true or not, can't recall nor would I have let her against my better judgment.

She came back with me regardless. At first, I took the back road to avoid detection but got impatient so at the halfway mark between New Rockford and Carrington by Barlow. As we turned onto the pavement, which was a bad judgment in general and/or even driving while intoxicated but had a high tolerance. I didn't feel the full effect of being drunk if that makes sense but I was tired that night too. This reminds me that Joshua could have had a high tolerance to alcohol as well and still able to function normally to the point, where he knew what he was doing the night he took my brother's life.

Anyways clearly history is about to repeat itself here, whether it was entrapment or not a car behind me had their bright lights on so I pulled over to let it pass. I never identified it as a police car till he or she activated their lights. If you remember back in 2012 another stop took place. I knew it was a cop and thought she'd go right by me if I pulled over. I can't remember all the details about this stop. I got cited for open container, so I didn't think to dump it out on the floor or anything. As this is happening, I was trying to plan ahead by calling my girlfriend but she wasn't answering resulting in myself getting angry and/or frustrated with her.

I ended up doing the sobriety test as well as the breathalyzer there and at the station. I was fully cooperating with them but for some reason they forgot to take a blood sample from me at the hospital. Maybe the breathalyzer at the police station replaced this either way, besides the bright light, it was a good arrest. Whether it was a setup and/or someone called me in I should have never been out there so of course they arrested, charged and released me. I think my sister drove my car to the station and waited for me. I don't recall if they tested her or not or if she had been drinking. While at the station doing breathalyzers and paperwork, they eventually released me on a promise to appear bond.

Now I am at home that's where I should have stayed, right? My blood was pumping though I was not ready to sleep it off and/or end the night after all the excitement I have had. My sister didn't wanna return my keys until the next day until I sobered up but eventually talked her into giving them to me. A mistake maybe? Yes, I ain't trying to nor can I justify my actions in any way that night. I ended up at my ex's. All I remembered is she claimed that she slept with another guy is how an argument started out. It never escalated more than that if I remember correctly but she called the cops. I then kept telling her I was leaving but she continued to stay on phone with them at this point.

She wasn't allowing me to go anywhere blocking her apartment door. I remember telling a cop I should have just moved her someway or did something but would have resulted in another charge. After sometime one cop maybe two responded but the one City Officer Nyguard took me out of the apartment then slamming me up against the wall handcuffing me. As he was taking me out, he was asking her if she wanted to press more charges against me like disorderly conduct, and she replied no.

The officer then patted me down while leaning against the car finding my keys then assuming I drove there, then charges me with another driving under the influence. I never admitted to driving I explained to him my sister drove my car there but he wasn't gonna buy it. Second one that night which would cost me a total of three thousand dollars. fifteen hundred for each of them, in order to fight them in court. Anyways, back to the office as they do another report and this time I am going to jail. I can't recall all of my actions, but I was making them nervous to the point where they would handcuff me to a chair and then transport me to jail with shackles on. I was slipping my handcuffs from back to front back in 2012 maybe it was related to that arrest.

On this second charge, I refused to blow knowing it would be thrown out and it was not justified but later would learn it was not up to the courts. Whether it was a change made to the law but from my understanding it was up to the department of transportation to decide it. At the end my license would be revoked for a total of five years—three years for the refusal. I was maybe in jail a night or two before initial appearance in court. If I remember correctly, I had to agree to wear a twenty-four seven alcohol bracelet as a bond release condition but before putting it on. I grabbed what I thought I should have at that time. I then only took Ladybird with me, since she was my first dog, then headed towards New Town where my mother worked and lived. Thinking back maybe I should have took all the dogs with but all I had on mind was to run at the time.

I know I should have dealt with the consequences better for my actions, but back then I couldn't see myself wearing a bracelet and being sober every day. I gave my mom a heads-up I was coming once I got there, I found her while she was working a shift. My anxiety was high at the time maybe from the drinking and/or running? I got set up there for a while still not learning from my mistakes started drinking everyday again but at least I had my car and Ladybird. I felt good being out of Carrington but soon a warrant would be issued for my arrest. Now I am fugitive from Carrington living on the reservation but my mom would say she enjoyed me being around. The casino was feeding my bad habits I would get lucky winning money from the casino. I would buy what I needed like cigarettes booze and gas then gambling with the rest. I didn't need much money for food cause my mom would bring what they were gonna throw out home with her.

Ladybird was getting spoiled eating sandwiches. I was killing two birds with one stone saving money on dog food and not letting it go to waste is how I saw it. I was buying strong booze called Evra Brooks it was ninety-proof good, cheap and got the job done but for some reason they quit stocking it. Could it have been because I was buying it all the time? It was weird though moved on to another brand then the same thing happened maybe they were being racist and/or trying to tell me to sober up? They could have just been lazy too and not ordered anymore.

Either way I was enjoying myself meeting this girl at the casino we would hang out together a lot. She wasn't really my type but wasn't too picky back then either. I'd drive my car with Ladybird by the water it felt so peaceful for some reason. Don't worry everything was close together so I wasn't drinking and driving as much, everything I needed was with then two miles of the area. Few times I did check out the library but was sober though if I went away from the area because I couldn't take any risks with getting caught. I'd learn later that the New Town police were able to arrest and transport me, even though I was white. At one point I made the mistake of returning to Carrington whether it was to see my little sister or check up on my dogs.

Also, during this point, I put my little sister's boyfriend in charge of taking care of the dogs and my trailer house during my absence from Carrington. I may have still been in contact with the ex at this time and may have gotten back together with her for a short period of time. Living with my friend Elmer remembering staying at the ex's for a few days is when I started watching the show *Fargo* at her place and/or maybe that took place earlier either way.

So, I get back to Carrington not sure if it was even a day that I was back in town before the cops came for me. All I remember was I had a few drinks with Amanda and her boyfriend, for some reason I am remember the drinks were mixed in five-gallon jug that was sitting on the water cooler. I am guessing he just loved his alcohol this much but he would always get sloppy drunk. This one time he pulled his pants down in front of my mom and just stood there thinking she would sleep with him? Shortly after visiting the police showed up.

He knew I had a warrant but still ran me through the radio. I was waiting for him to turn his head so I could run, but I attempted to slowly sneak away. He caught this, of course. Whether I was getting tired and old of this I never ran but as a precaution he handcuffed me warrant confirmed. I told Amanda my sister and her estranged boyfriend to take care of Ladybird. Sister's boyfriend got a funny idea in his head claiming I told him to transfer my car into his name, while I was in jail. He further claimed the now sheriff of Carrington was a witness to this. Sometime after this I called to confirm, but they refused and was more interested in knowing my location. So, I may have told 'em I was over at my sister's trailer. They went over there to search for me, of course.

After that, my sister and her boyfriend were mad at me for a while. I thought it was funny at the time. Amanda described it as a few officers going inside to search and a deputy waiting outside of the door to handcuff me. I have not had contact with the boyfriend since then. Whether it was a shitty thing to do something I would regret that happened. When we made it to the jail, they never breathalyzed me so I was among the general population still feeling good tell I woke up sober. Must have spent seven days in jail. During that time, my ex slapped Elmer to the point where he saw stars. I was released agreed to wearing the bracelet again and for the time being. I had seven days to decide what to do because they would check it once a week.

Around June 2017 all this is taking place. I was thinking about playing it straight but was not ready to be sober so I cut the bracelet off leaving it in the shed. I couldn't return it, right? Or I would have ended up in jail right then and there. Somehow made it back to New Town with my dog, of course. Couldn't take my car with cause of license being revoked and apparently selling it to my sisters goofy boyfriend. Thinking about it when he was under the influence, he would always have this giggle, when telling a story. Now if true that I sold him my car he would have taken advantage of my mind while under the influence, but if I was as drunk, why couldn't the police and/or correctional officers tell?

Somehow, I ended back in New Town. Eventually Carrington issued another warrant so I was a wanted man yet again. At some point I got mixed up with the wrong crowd this one guy told me to wait at the Casino door while he stole a bag of potato chips, while he was running out, he told me to run as well following natural instinct I did but made me look guilty. He outran me, so I got caught and questioned; never told them much just explained what I knew. They wanted to search my mom's recreational vehicle for him so I had to give my mom a heads-up. They never found him in there, of course.

Whether they ran my name can't say but thinking if they did the warrant would pop up another close call. My first close call was when me and my mother went to a powwow we got stopped for speeding. Police never did ask for my identification though but he did make me dump out my open container due to it ain't legal and pow woos don't allow alcohol after this we just turned around and went back.

Anyways never got charged with anything or banned from casino that night, until I walked in there pushing my luck again ended up being detained in the casino jail for a bit. They decided to ban me for thirty days but I continued to push my luck ninety days still continued and it was a year ban with a strong warning that they would call the cops next time. After this I never attempted again because I didn't wanna take the risk of course with the police you know what they say third time would be the charm that will play a role as we continue into it.

Right around this time a Chuck came in the picture he was working in oilfields as a wielder not only was he working on dating my mom but also worked on getting me a job with the connections he had but was unsuccessful whether it was lack of experience drinking and/or both played a role in it. I was always shaky and nervous for multiple reasons. Chuck would bring us out to dinner and his camper where he took a picture of my mom that he framed.

She didn't want it so I took it but she wasn't interested in him for her own personal reasons whether it was her still grieving over her lost husband that she lost in 2012 and/or was not her type but he did have money offering to pay for a lawyer to fight my case. Lawyers plan for three thousand dollars was to get first one dropped and second one lowered to a reckless driving. Reason for finding this lawyer in a way he found me saw my case on the public court record site sent me mail. For some reason Chuck only paid half fifteen hundred nonrefundable before he could pay the other half, he got mad at my mother at the time could have been because he thought someone was using the white pickup he had got for her. My brother would punch it for some reason creating a dent.

Chucks suspicions would later be confirmed by me. I remembered having a talk with him telling me not to **** with him as far as I know I never have, just a random thought that popped in. How they met you ask? My mom was working as a Porter also known as a janitor at the casino. He would tip her using a hundred-dollar bill, so in a way he basically was trying to buy her. To this day last I heard he was working somewhere in Oklahoma.

Around this time, Big D comes back in my life, he was coming to New Town to sell food for the pow woo where I offered to help at this point. His only rule he had for me while staying or working for him was no drinking. I did tell him I would bring Ladybird with me he agreed. Remembering the pow woo at four bears in New Town was slow so it was not bad for me getting back in the game once again. When I worked with him, I pretty much was his second in command and/or his right-hand man. If I didn't include it, he was one reason I started to dress to impress and for success.

He always wore colored dress shirts with ties never afraid of getting them dirty and/or doing the work no one else wanted to do. I picked up good traits he had and was also keeping me sober I was surprised I wasn't drinking at the time, that he knew of maybe sneaked a shot or two but that was it, no heavy drinking. He told me I had a lazy mind which is active whether because of him and/or my federal trip. Anyways we got pow woo done with at four bears. My mom let him use the white pick to transport a food stand, which I was the driver of it.

I never towed anything like this in my life only reason why I remember it so well cause it was scary I wasn't paying close attention while pulling it nor was I giving a heads up. Anyways I start noticing something called sway control flashing luckily this was a new pickup, right? If it was older maybe food wagon would have rolled me because it was swaying all over the road. I ended up pulling over and trying to center everything thinking we ended up moving at a slower speed in order to maintain control. We were heading towards Fort Peck another powwow and/or one in Poplar not sure which one came first. This was on the eastern side of Montana little over a two-hundred-mile drive.

Let's say Fort Peck came first. When we set up Big D always wanted everything to be perfect. We would have to level the stands using bricks and blocks of wood, then hooking up the water after that the electricity, there were always problems with it for some reason. There would be two stands the one used for drinks and the other for food.

Then we organized, if necessary, then started selling food early. Big D was greedy how I saw it and/or cared a lot about costumer service. He would wanna open up for business for one person but this would always stress me out. The hardest part I thought when I had a lazy mind was the setup, teardown, and cleaning up, but now I am trained to do what needs to get done.

Nothing happened to Ladybird at this powwow that I recall usually I'd keep her safe from other dogs by keeping her in the camper thinking she was in heat at this time. Can't remember specific details about this one, but the other powwow in Poplar I had put Ladybird in the camper. I was busy working when she got out. Big D's hateful wife was the one that let her louse and that's when Ladybird engaged or was raped by another dog I remember keeping this husky dog away from the food stand he was big and Ladybird was small medium dog. Thinking if he got on her he'd kill her from the sex whether it sounds silly or not this was my fear, which eventually became a reality. After the powwow, I went looking for her remember seeing blood. Thinking it was from the dog and she was dead.

After looking for a while, I returned to the food wagon and started grieving over her loss thinking the worst of course. After sometime I came out was walking around and saw her she was walking like a zombie not responding to my voice wobbling back and forth. I don't know if she was gang raped by dogs or just this one husky did it. Again, I know it sounds silly to read or hear, but it was bad. I had mixed emotions about this, of course, blaming Big D's wife. Ladybird was puking bad, but luckily, she recovered from it. To this day I am sure she didn't get killed because of her being pregnant maybe? This will be explained further later on as the last powwow was over I wanted to take a break but Big D wanted us to clean up right after.

This never happened instead I drank and told a secret to his friends and/or my coworkers the reason his wife hated me. Secret was that I slept with her they couldn't believe it and were surprised. I started talking and came up with another escape plan. Ended up getting a ride to wolf point somehow remembering being at someone's house. Thinking he was someone I met while working at the powwow then getting a hotel room one that allowed dogs. While she was puking everywhere I was thinking of my next move.

My mom ended up picking us up and then returning to New Town for a short period of time. Sometime during my stay here, I started reading documents from my past when I was a child that included custody battles with the courts in Rapid City, South Dakota, Military court records involving my brother James and other documents related to family matters. I don't know why this stuff is important to include here but remember a letter I found that I wrote to James while he was serving overseas. He wanted me to send him booze disguised as mouth wash through the mail whether this happened or not. I cannot confirm it but at the time he was underage so he couldn't buy booze. I'd like to think him being in the service helped shape him up putting him on a good path like what my federal experience did for me.

Sure, I was still drinking after returning but my crimes were down. Remembering our old Sunday school teacher Gail attending the funeral service I was surprised. According to public court records James made a payment to his fines on July 1st, 2008 would someone suicidal pay their fines? Did he see something that day? April maybe something of interest? I don't know why this came up at this time but it's here. Here I started talking with an old coworker that I worked with. She was single. Yeah, I was thinking with my other head here. Again, I was making plans to see her. She was not too bright but attractive. She and her other sister were twins, both working at a truck-stop but lacking common sense. One was smarter than the other.

They were told to card people that looked like they were under twenty-seven but instead they carded everyone for cigarettes even if they looked ninety years old. Earlier my boss wanted me on their shift told her. If she did, that better give me a raise instead she moved me to graveyard shift in return getting a dollar raise for overnight differential and good coworkers as well so good another win there. Sisters would as I'd call it mind **** me the stuff they would come up with. A mind ****ing included not thinking straight needing a long break from them. Thinking smoking meth may have made them this way but hard to say for sure.

Anyways she was located in a town near Carrington, and yes, I was drinking this day but my mom let me take her car for good it would turn out to be. I took Ladybird with, of course. I was being impatient than was speeding when I got pulled over. I was a mile or two away from the casino. Police officer then performed a sobriety test I surprisingly pass it but puts me in his car that's when I heard over the radio that my warrant was confirmed. I asked officer if he would drop my dog off with my mom, he claimed he would but instead called animal control. He filed new charges against me for that area. I'd later miss court and they would ask if I wanted to reschedule. I never did because I was thinking warrant would be local only based on the fact of them allowing me to reschedule. He kept on trying to get me to bribe him or something.

Officer claimed I could pay off my fine and/or post a bail for current and/or other charges even going as far as asking if I wanted him to give my mom some money. Maybe if I went with the third option id still have my dog but who knows how much things would have changed whether for the better and/or good. People say everything happens for a reason either way we were both in the wrong that day as I see it. On top of that he had the car towed claiming it was suspicious and/or may have been involved in a crime. He or another officer then transported me and another to the nearest white county jail. My mom claimed she went to pick my dog up but they wanted some kind of documentation like a birth certificate? Are you kidding me? Come on. This is one reason that discourages me from donating to animal shelters again. Two wrongs shouldn't make it right, though?

Now I was in jail officer never gave me my Identification back later calling them to mail it. At first, they claimed to not have any knowledge of it but after a while it randomly showed up at an old address. After a few hours sitting in the Mountrail County Jail, a Foster County deputy showed up wanting to handcuff me in back but said no because it was gonna be a long ride, then he said, "I'll have to shackle you." I said, "Okay that will work," but he must have had a soft heart that day and/or I called his bluff because he just handcuffed me up front. I was transported to Ramsey County Jail in Devils Lake, North Dakota, whether it was the closest one or it was their main at the time, I don't know. But I had a bail hearing; state's attorney was not present I do believe it was set at three hundred cash.

I was deciding concerned whether I should bail out and/or wait on my court appearance, knowing after the fact I should have waited but at this time I had no idea what the officer did with my dog. I was hoping Ladybird was back with my mom, so I bailed out taking the risk of being thrown back in, others were thinking id be back they would be right.

I quickly cashed my check at a store then buying cigarettes, booze and then contacting my sister to pick me up. As I waited smoking my cigarettes and drinking, not even thinking to get ahold of my mom, but of course when you're in jail it stuns and/or disorientates you. When walking out, your changing environments if that makes sense and/or nicotine withdraw also played a role. Yes, drinking didn't help any.

Once I got picked up went to New Rockford staying overnight at a friend's and continuing to drink staying up late when I had court the next day. Yes, a bad idea and/or judgment soon would pay for it. I was deciding whether I should skip court or not ended up doing the right thing for once in my life. I could have went on the run again then picking my dog up but choose to trust the courts. As I got there, I saw Paul. He indicated that he smelled booze on my breath, then him instructing me to take a breathalyzer with the sheriff. Apparently, I was still under the influence breathalyzed then handcuffed had to wait to sober up before I could see the judge.

State's attorney explained that I was most likely a functional alcoholic. I am afraid that he was correct whether this helped or hurt hard to say. I remember sitting up in the sheriff's office having coffee and donuts trying to sober up. I ended up puking, which probably helped a lot now sober and ready. Before I go on I'll point out I realize how much I messed up but what I am about to tell or write you it won't make it better or more right. Furthermore, does not justify state's attorney's actions. A few people before or after me appeared were released on a personal recognizance bond, basically means no bail required. While I was the only that went back to jail. Thinking I was still under influence, while a plea deal was worked out. Whether this was legal or not? I only did the plea deal to have my freedom, if I would have knowing what was gonna take place next, I would have fought it. Thinking everything is gonna be fine now that I did the plea deal, I then called my sister to bring the bracelet I cut off. Earlier a woman found it in the shed why she was looking around in here I don't know, but I cooperated with them.

It's my turn. Plea deal judge approves. Paul then files theft of property class c felony, criminal mischief class A misdemeanor then requests a high bail. Now does it make any sense for me to steal a twenty-four seven alcohol bracelet? Criminal mischief charge makes more sense but my intention was to get it off my angle not cause any damage. I could have simply paid for it instead of going this route. I argue against the bail telling them I gotta get my dog, which I only had three days before they would shoot or adopt her out. Judge went in favor of the state's attorney for me to be held with bail.

I can't remember how much bail was but knew I would be in jail for a while cause I wouldn't be able to pay it. The deputy that transported me wasn't a smoker but offered to buy me a mellow yellow. I gladly accepted it again I returned to Ramsey County Jail other inmates were laughing at or with me. I soon got a jail job working in the kitchen it was sweet got all the milk I wanted and extra food trays but this would throw my sleep off. While in there would also work out, write letters to my friend Elmer, which I always write him when I am incarceration-ed even when I had that federal trip. Remembering him saying you don't have to go to jail just to write

me. We couldn't go outside because they were fixing the fencing due to a few inmates escaping. One female guard was nice she printed me of my dead brother's mug shot. I would later take picture of both of our mugshots together and use it as a cover on mugbook.

She knew me somehow whether it was word of mouth or

mutual friends but she did live in New Rockford after a while there was a bail reduction hearing I requested for myself. My lawyer was asking me how much I could pay thinking I said five hundred never posted it. Shortly after I appeared in court a plea deal was worked out total days in jail served were twenty-nine. At court plea deal was signed off on for a reason they did not release me right there and then took me back to jail where I had to sit. I was waiting for paperwork to come through was getting impatience kept telling the guards to keep checking on it. At this time my sister was at the jail waiting for me but ended up leaving because they told her I had a hold from Eddy County which is located in New Rockford.

When they came and told me this my reaction was priceless it was like a wow one but told them they were wrong last crime I committed there was back in 2012. I continued to tell them it was a mistake and I already gave my spot away in jail after waiting longer. I said **** it and found another spot like it was a Chicago all over again. After what felt like a few hours, they finally realized their mistake but never explained it that I can recall but was very upset wanted to file a complaint against them never did file one due to the fact I forgot about it until now.

Funny thing entering or leaving a jail is like entering a different zone once you leave you may forget about what took place in there. Luckily another inmate was going through the same thing so I was able to catch a ride back with her. When I did call my sister, she told me what happened and was already back in New Rockford, which is about a forty-minute drive one way. While we walked around trying find a place to cash my check one store quit doing it for some reason. Another reason I wanted my mug shot with my jail information was because I had no identification to confirm my age. Eventually her friend arrived we got booze chatted until I got dropped off in New Rockford again.

Thinking next day I was back in Carrington staying at Elmer's place making phone calls trying to find out what happened to Ladybird. call after call person after person nothing this is what they basically told me. She is either in a shelter or is dead but used their light killing term—*euthanized*. Okay? Which one is it? She's either dead or in a shelter. Okay? Like did I abuse her? reason they can't tell me where to find my dog? I recall a time I was at a library in New Town thinking this woman was crazy. She was saying people kidnapped dogs to eat them or some other reason. Hmm... maybe she was right?

Anyways I was frustrated blamed not only New Town but the Foster County state's attorney and also myself. I remember the state's attorney asking me to confess or pay for his window saying he knew it was me but couldn't poof it once AGAIN. I put out posters online to find her this one site told me they would not get involved because of the circumstances surrounding the police. Again, did I abuse her or something? Maybe acting like she's a child taking away because of neglect? Yes, I considered her as a daughter but am pretty sure she is a dog. So, I was at a loss, like why are they making it so hard? Kept trying, trying, trying but never found her.

At this time, I returned to my job at Casey's my dog was gone a loss I suffered because of my actions and others playing their fair share of roles in my life. Another loss I was gonna take was my close coworker Michael. He was planning on moving to Fargo to be closer to his family whether this was his only motive or others were involved, I cannot recall and only person that would know is himself. He was considering to stay if the company gave him a raise this never happened but he deserved a big one. Michael was a modeled employee except for being ten minutes late for almost every shift other than that he never missed one, if he could help it. This is the problem with employers they never keep the good ones, reason why my job history is so sketchy but he was still with the company just transferred to another store. Ladybird now him gone things were not the same sometime after I saw an old jail friend passing through living in Minot at the time now deceased.

Those that don't remember he was involved in an accident

slash murder case. Checked for updates on him still none whether it was him setting off triggers or not. I couldn't say what was bothering me whether it involved the past and/or current losses can't really say. I started having my first panic attack at work, felt like I couldn't breathe; stomach muscles were sore from being tensed up. I remembered talking to my boss and/or another coworker explaining it and then moved to the deli to see if it would help ease it but never did. I can't recall if it was that exact day or after but I had my mind set that once I was clocked out id never return again. To this day I never did go back inside the store to buy anything, whether it was the guilt, shame, loss and/or everything in general with the area hitting me all at once. No matter how silly it sounds. To this day I view Carrington as a war zone.

I ended up at Elmer's house on his couch soaking myself in a bottle fueled by an endless depression trip. I was paying for all my food, booze, cigarettes and then some in return helping him out. Eventually he got upset with me can't or don't wanna remember why. Thinking he just wanted to be alone again but he was willing to get into a fight resulting in myself gathering what I could including my booze. In my tire-slashing days, I would have engaged but I was a changed person. I know what you're thinking like wow grabbing the booze when you gonna learn guy?

Whether losing Ladybird was another turning point and/or a rock bottom as I did hit one several times in my life changed me and/or continued to direct me on a better path. I ended taking my stuff next door to Bonnie's even she didn't wanted me there feeling sad that I was getting rejected by her too. I knew I couldn't stand outside because it was winter during this period. She finally let me in after several knocks at door then started drinking some beers with her talking and figuring out my next move. I then called my sister Amanda her and Frank agreed to take me to Jamestown.

The plan was to stay with my father, Bill, the guy that considers me to be his son and married to my mom. I remember that drive he was texting at same time scared me a bit. I would have left Carrington sooner but felt trapped there because no one would transport me there. At one time I was calling the cops on myself in hopes that they would take me to Jamestown for being drunk in public but my plan backfired instead there was a rumor created that I was trying to kill cops. The rumor made was false.

My drinking was so bad I couldn't even see my sister sober. I'd be uncontrollably shaking. I was a decrease, deserving not to be alive, a complete mess and failed in life is what I thought of myself at the time. While at my father's place (whether it's weird to play into it or not) my drinking continued. While being in Jamestown I couldn't even interact with a cashier at Walmart my paranoia, anxiety, and shaking was that bad. After some time here I started to research, attempting to locate Ben my counselor and/or shrink from 2008-2009. I eventually found him on shrinkbook then started to message him. I should have saw him earlier but I remember times I would attempt to track him down but they were all unsuccessful and/or I wasn't ready to see him. Ben's last name was hard to spell.

Whether the reasons this time I was ready to see him again. It was hard to do the right thing, which was to confront myself and seek out help, it needed to be done.

I was breaking up with the love of my life or what I thought it was to be, alcohol was one thing that never left and was always there. We have been through everything together the good, the bad and the ugly and now it was time to start distancing myself from it. Before I could come into the treatment, they wanted me to check myself in the state hospital for detox but I was already there and I wasn't playing around. Basically said you take me in and/or I'll just go back and drink, they then took me in. I ended up detoxing in there for a few days before I could join the group. I was in bad shape shaking in front of my trusted counselor. Remembering him telling me I was safe here and/or something along those lines not sure if I was emotionally unstable, scared to change and/or shaking from the booze. Before this other treatment, I have had that I can remember was two taking place in Cando 2008-2009 Fargo 2015 and now Rolla 2018. Speaking of treatments, I have been in seven different county jails in North Dakota, that I can remember.

So, I just voluntarily enrolled myself into treatment in Rolla, North Dakota at this time I wasn't paying my fines didn't want my treatment interrupted so I had my counselor fax or send a letter to the courts stating I was enrolled in the program. I remember this book we had to fill out every day it involved sharing a person's thoughts. One day I wrote I hated myself remembering Ben saying that was a strong feeling. I'd hate to bring myself down at this point of my writing but look at who I was back starting in 2008 or even 2011. I was a complete monster looking back I wouldn't wanna know or be around that person.

That person is myself Yes. I hate that person he was a horrible he didn't care about no body but himself. Look where he is at now; he's here shaking in treatment. Why did he take so long to change??? Why did anyone wanna be involved with him? He didn't value his family, mom, dog, left his dad to die alone, while drinking at a bar. He had a best friend from childhood where is he GONE. He had a positive father figure Big D but he goes and sleeps with his girlfriend, while he is stuck in jail because of him being selfish. Who would not hate this person? This person is better off dead. This person again is me.

My counselor would later describe these as intense feelings. We were able to smoke outside of course my mom was helping me out by sending me money to buy cigarettes. They allowed us to walk around town for exercise and/or other reasons. I should have not been able to leave at all. You can probably guess why. if you were thinking I went and got some booze you were right, not sure how long I was here before doing this but it only hurt me more and/or my progress that I made. I can't remember if I confessed this to him yet but one of the workers in charge of watching us, she found out because I was sloppy covering it up. I wish she would have told but instead said nothing about it.

After I did this I was wondering what is wrong with me? I came here to get help and here I was drinking wasting not only my time but there's as well. I also was back on medication while here but didn't like taking them anymore because I felt like a zombie with my balls cut off. I started skipping my pills pocketing them for this I was eventually caught, when caught my face lit up red. Turned out someone before me got caught if I remember right, it was an older lady her voice and look made me feel ashamed of myself.

Thinking at this point I started realizing that my feelings were catching up to me after soaking and/or suppressing them with booze for so many years. The only time I was sober was if I was incarceration-ed and/or working at a job. I was feeling remorseful for my actions. When we had group, he asked about the pills. I explained and then he pointed out to me that I could have just refused them but I was not thinking about that option at the time and/or I wanted him to keep thinking I was doing good. I wanted to do a one-on-one session with him so bad in exchange I could have a good cry. Just like the first time but he was always busy nor did I push it as much either. I just didn't believe I deserved any help, another person in the group made crying look easy. There were a few times that the dam holding back loads of tears was about to bust open, which reminds me I would shed tears walking down a street thinking I was the only one that noticed it. I would describe my hurt and/or sadness as a dam holding back water that dam was cracking water would slowly leak out.

I can't recall everything and/or choose not include it all that took place here whether it's still hard to process or I am ashamed of myself. The staff were supportive met a girl in there but never became more than just a co-client. I remember Ben saying people only contacted him when they are doing bad, so now I call him at least once a week rather I am doing good or bad. I asked permission to use his real name in this writing but choose not to because I don't want his voicemail blowing up. Reason I call him Ben is cause of my favorite movie analyze this and that. I felt like that gangsta for some reason and the shrink would help Paul even though he was a mess and involved in crime. Being here directed me closer to being reformed.

After more time passing, they felt that it was time for me to leave but I wanted to stay though. I wasn't opening up like I should have been. You can help a person support them but at the end of the day it gonna be up to them not you. One thing I told my mom after she told me to quit drinking, the more she talked about it the more I would do it. I remember her slapping me a few times; of course, I deserved it, though.

I had a ride lined up for Bill to pick me up and return to Jamestown. I had a court appearance that I requested to appear by phone because I didn't wanna go back there. The judge denied my request then issuing a warrant for my arrest. While having this active warrant people would ask about it but would never be truthful and I still continued attending alcoholics anonymous. Alcoholics anonymous was another turning around point for me. I never believed in it but was in a good supportive group. This is also when I met Bud; he was friends with Bill both attending alcoholics anonymous. I wasn't drinking doing my best to stay sober. Yes, there were a few times I would drink but it wasn't as bad and never enjoyed it. Big D would say have a drink to enjoy it I wasn't one that couldn't just have one beer and be done through the next writing? I would eventually get to that point though. When Bill invited Bud over, I was nervous not that he was a bad guy but being around someone sober I wasn't used to it nor was I taking any medication so it was a challenge for me. I described it earlier as being a dog meeting a new person for the first time.

This may be the point when I start eating healthier and/or noticing how much alcohol was affecting my health like my hair. I was and still am determinant to be a better person then I ever was. One good thing about Alcoholics Anonymous is they had coffee, tea and other people struggling with addiction. No matter the addictions- gambling, alcohol, drugs, air duster, cough medicine, paint and others. We all have a different choice of a drug to use but what we all have in common is using them to escape, deal with our emotions and/or other reasons or excuses we use to justify our own use. While living in Jamestown, I didn't have a bad setup, a good group of supportive friends.

I got to the point where I never wanted to miss a alcoholics anonymous meeting. Readers that are not familiar with it every group would be different. I have not gone through all and/or one step that I know of but it came in my life at the right time. The group I was in was perfect others may take it to an extreme though so if you're interested continue to attending meetings, until tell you find one you like.

Surround yourself with people that have a sense of humor. The fun we had using our choice of drug can also be done sober. Revisit your hometown and/or past which can include old friends, things and places. Travel visit or live in another area it's scary I know because I have been there. Once your mind is set in a negative setting, you don't see the positives, just the negatives. if I would have noticed this about myself earlier could have had more time. Your body will create fear because it ain't used to the change. Everyone is scared of change and/or someone different but these battles we must overcome and succeed. No one would ever believe who I am today how much I have changed for the better. I am not saying the world is a good place but acknowledge it put it in the back of your mind until you can do something about it.

I myself struggle with balance I caught myself not seeing the negative actions in a relationship I was only focused on the positive side. I go with the flow due to plans always go backwards and/or falling apart. There is a purpose for us all but we must find it and not drown our self in a bottle of alcohol cough medicine and/or paint. We must not smoke our self in a cloud of marijuana meth and/or other drugs. Yes, marijuana is legal in most states, but alcohol is legal in all of them. I have saw people go crazy smoking marijuana whether it was laced and/or fake.

To this day I am still recovering from so many years of neglect to myself. Thirty years old, no matter your age it is never too late to change yourself and/or to make improvements. It took three years of anger before noticeable depression setting in 2011. Our past is never easy to process, better to live in the present in order to create a better future.

Thank you for reading my book. I hope my life experience can make a positive impact on yours It was a challenge going back in my mind mentally but was able to kill two birds with one stone. While writing this, I have experienced dreams, mixed emotions, and depression, but I have finished it.

A Human

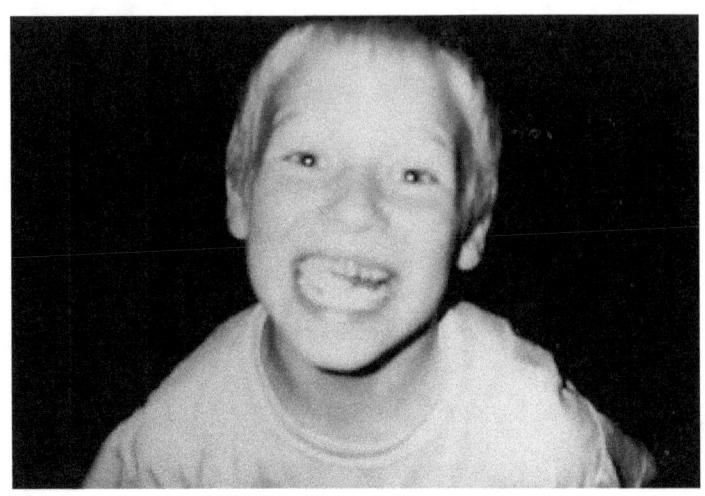

A Building

A Rising Stock

Feedback, Concerns, Questions?
Email: ahumannowunpredictable@gmail.com

www.ingramcontent.com/pod-product-compliance
Lightning Source LLC
LaVergne TN
LVHW011841060526
838200LV00054B/4126